SPAIN

SPAIN

A SHINING NEW DEMOCRACY

DISCOVERING our HERITAGE

by Geraldine Woods

DILLON PRESS, INC.
Minneapolis, Minnesota 55415

Library of Congress Cataloging in Publication Data

Woods, Geraldine.
Spain : a shining new democracy.

(Discovering our heritage)
Bibliography: p.
Includes index.
Summary: Contrasts Spain's past of castles, Moorish invaders, and fair ladies with today's fast-growing democracy, featuring such cultural aspects as schools, sports, food, and folktales.
1. Spain—Juvenile literature. [1. Spain]
I. Title. II. Series.
DP17.W59 1987 946.083 86-30935
ISBN 0-87518-340-5

Dillon Press, Inc., 242 Portland Avenue South
Minneapolis, Minnesota 55415

Printed in the United States of America
1 2 3 4 5 6 7 8 9 10 96 95 94 93 92 91 90 89 88 87

Contents

Acknowledgments

The author thanks Silvia Defior, Mariano Moles, Vanesa Moles, and Vital Moles for their help with this book.

Photographic Acknowledgments

The photographs are reproduced through the courtesy of the Carmel Mission Gift Shop; Collection, The Museum of Modern Art, New York, Mrs. Simon Guggenheim Fund, Pablo Picasso, Three Musicians, *1921 (summer), oil on canvas, 6'7" x 7'3-3/4" (200.7 x 222.9 cm.); Robert Fried (©1987, cover and pages 10, 23, 39, 44, 47, 99, 109, 117, 124, 130, 146); Milt and Joan Mann—Cameramann International (©1987, pages 29, 118, 129); the National Tourist Office of Spain; Carla R. Phillips; Reuters/Bettmann Newsphotos, page 31; Rogers and Cowan, Inc.; Robert Royal—Creative Edge Photography (©1987, pages 41, 103, 127); Royce Carlton, Inc.; Tom Stack and Associates—Steve Elmore (© 1987, page 87); UPI/Bettmann Newsphotos, page 67.*

Fast Facts About Spain

Official Name: *Estado Español.*

Capital: Madrid.

Location: Western Europe. Spain occupies most of the Iberian Peninsula and includes the Canary and Balearic Islands. Portugal is to the west and France to the east. To the north is the North Atlantic Ocean and the Bay of Biscay, and to the south is the Mediterranean Sea.

Area: 194,890 square miles (about 504,750 square kilometers). Spain extends 646 miles (1,040 kilometers) from east to west, and 547 miles (880 kilometers) from north to south. It has 2,345 miles (3,774 kilometers) of coastline.

Elevation: *Highest*—The Mulhacén, in the Sierra Nevada, 11,411 feet (3,478 meters) above sea level. *Lowest*—Sea level along the coast.

Population: 39,300,000. *Distribution*—91 percent urban, 9 percent rural. *Density*—200 persons per square mile (about 80 per square kilometer).

Form of Government: Parliamentary monarchy. A king is the head of state, but the prime minister is the head of the government.

Some Important Products: Cars, ships, leather, chemicals, cement, steel, shoes, clothing; oranges, wheat, olives, lemons, oats, rye, wool, grapes; wine, sherry.

Basic Unit of Money: Peseta.

Languages: Castilian Spanish is the official language, but Catalan, Galician, and Euskera (Basque) are also recognized.

Religion: Spain is 99 percent Roman Catholic.

Flag: Three horizontal panels of red, gold, and red, with the national coat of arms in the center gold panel.

National Anthem: "Himno Nacional" (National Anthem).

Some Major Holidays: Catholic feasts of Christmas (December 25); Day of the Three Kings (January 6); Holy Week (date varies); as well as many individual saints' days; New Year's Day (January 1); Students' Day (January 28); Civil War Anniversary (July 18); and Hispanic Day (October 12).

Spanish Provinces: Spain is divided into fifty provinces, which are grouped into seventeen "autonomous regions." The autonomous regions have powers similar to those of the American states.

Bay of Biscay
FRANCE
ASTURIAS
GALICIA
CANTABRIA
CANTABRIAN MOUNTAINS
Bilbao
BASQUE
NAVARRE
PYRENEES MOUNTAINS
CASTILE-LEÓN
LA RIOJA
Ebro River
Duero River
PORTUGAL
SPAIN
Zaragoza
CATALONIA
SIERRA DE GUADARRAMA
Madrid
ARAGON
Barcelona
Costa Brava
Tajo River
MADRID
ESTREMADURA
Guadiana River
CASTILE-LA MANCHA
VALENCIA
Valencia
BALEARIC ISLANDS
SIERRA MORENA
Guadalquivir River
Seville
ANDALUSIA
MURCIA
TH ATLANTIC OCEAN
Costa Blanca
Málaga
SIERRA NEVADA
Mediterranean Sea
Strait of Gilbraltar
GIBRALTAR (Great Britain)
Costa del Sol
MOROCCO
ALGERIA
N
CANARY ISLANDS
AFRICA
NORTH AMERICA
SPAIN
EUROPE
ASIA
AFRICA
SOUTH AMERICA
AUSTRALIA

1. The Hide of a Bull

Near Barcelona there is a mountain called Tibidabo. *Tibi dabo* means "I give this to you." According to a Bible story, this is what the devil said to Jesus when they were standing on top of a mountain. The devil was offering Jesus all the lands and riches in sight in exchange for Jesus' soul. Although the Bible story is clearly set in the Middle East, Barcelona's mountain is named Tibidabo anyway. It seems that Spaniards feel their land is lovely enough to be a temptation for anyone—even God!

Perhaps that is an exaggeration, but there is no doubt that Spain is beautiful. Its area makes it the third largest country in Europe. Spain occupies most of the Iberian Peninsula, a nearly square block of land at the western edge of Europe. Portugal lies along the Atlantic coast of the peninsula, and France borders eastern Spain. The ancient Romans, who once ruled these countries, referred to the Iberian Peninsula as "the hide of a bull" because they thought the shape of the peninsula was similar to that of a cattle skin stretched out to dry. To the north of this "hide" is the North Atlantic and the Bay of Biscay, and to the south is the Mediterranean Sea.

Spain's beautiful countryside includes plains, low hills, and mountains.

The dry plateau called the Meseta stretches across most of the Iberian Peninsula.

Two groups of islands are also part of Spain. The Balearic Islands lie in the Mediterranean Sea to the east of Spain. They consist of five large islands and a number of smaller ones. Majorca, Minorca, and Ibiza are the three largest Balearics. The thirteen Canary Islands are in the Atlantic Ocean about sixty miles from northwest Africa. The Canary Islands form two separate Spanish provinces.

Most of the Iberian Peninsula is a high, flat plateau called the *Meseta*, or "little table." Seen from the air, the Meseta is a rolling patchwork in thousands of shades of brown and gold with only small patches of green. On this plateau, the flat areas are not very fertile and are divided by hills and mountains. The region's weather is sunny for most of the year—pleasant for people, but very dry for farming. Summers are extremely hot on the Meseta and, despite the sun, winters are fairly cold.

Not all of Spain is dry, though. The wettest part of the country, Galicia, occupies the northwest corner of the peninsula. (The Romans named this area *Finisterre*—"the end of the earth"—before America was discovered.) It rains in Galicia almost every day, and a fine, mysterious-looking mist covers the ground on many mornings. Galicia has many green fields and long stretches of marshlands.

Cutting through the Meseta are several mountain chains called *sierras*, a word meaning "saws." The Sierra Morena, Sierra Nevada, and Sierra de Guadarrama are the most important. Spain's highest peak, the Mulhacén, is located in the Sierra Nevada. The Galician, Cantabrian, and Pyrenees mountain ranges run across the northern edge of Spain. Spain has so many mountains that it is the second highest European country after Switzerland. The Meseta is also crisscrossed by a number of important rivers, including the Guadalqui-

Several rugged mountain ranges cut through the Meseta.

vir, the Ebro, the Duero, the Tajo, and the Guadiana. These rivers supply much of the water used for irrigating crops in regions bordering the Meseta.

Spain is famous throughout the world for its Mediterranean coastline. The *Costa del Sol*, or "coast of the sun," is located in southern Spain; its name describes its weather perfectly. White, sandy beaches there attract many visitors. The *Costa Brava,* or "fierce coast," is also an appropriate title for the shoreline along the Mediterranean near France. The area is filled with high cliffs and jagged rocks that lie next to a sparkling blue sea.

An Isolated Nation

Recently a campaign to attract tourists to Spain used the slogan, "Spain is different." More than a hundred years earlier, the Emperor Napoleon of France put it another way when he said, "Europe ends at the Pyrenees." Although both statements are exaggerations, each is partly true. Spain's customs, history, and attitudes have traditionally been very different from those of other European countries.

This difference may be due to the fact that Spain's geography is full of natural barriers. Only three hundred miles of border link Spain to the European continent, and all of those miles are filled with the rugged Pyrenees Mountains. Spain's other mountain ranges run between many coastal areas and the interior Meseta. Also, many Spanish rivers, because of rapids or low water levels, cannot be used by large ships. Before modern methods of travel were invented, it was hard for Spaniards to travel out of their country and for foreigners to enter it. Aside from the waves of invaders that pierced the country's defenses from time to time, Spain remained apart from the rest of the continent throughout its history.

Spain's mountain barriers also helped to isolate one region of the country from another. Many Spaniards refer to their nation as "my Spain"—a sign of the personal pride they feel for their country. However, most Spaniards don't personally think of themselves as Spaniards. Instead, they identify themselves by the particular area in which they were born. They sometimes refer to this area as their *patria chica*, "little homeland."

Most of these patria chicas were independent kingdoms at some point in Spanish history. Through the years they were forged into one nation, divided into provinces, and later grouped into larger units called autonomous (self-governing) regions. Perhaps because of their respect for tradition, most Spaniards ignore these newer divisions in everyday speech. If a native of Salamanca is asked where he or she comes from, the answer will probably not be "Castile-León," the name of the autonomous region formed in 1981. Instead, the reply is likely to be "Old Castile," the name of the kingdom formed during the Middle Ages. These traditional regions of Spain each developed distinct ways of living.

The two Castiles, Old and New, give their name to the official language of Spain, Castilian. Castilian is

Modern Madrid is the largest city of Spain and a major business center.

considered by many to be the purest form of Spanish. It is easy to recognize because the letters *c* and *z* are often pronounced as if they were *th*'s. In Latin American and other forms of Spanish, *c*'s and *z*'s are pronounced as an *s*. (Appendix A is a guide to pronouncing Castilian Spanish.)

Most of Castile is located on the Meseta, and with the help of irrigation, the area has become an important agricultural region. Because Madrid, the capital and largest city of Spain, is located in New Castile, the area is also a major business center. Almost all of Spain's large companies and banks, as well as many foreign businesses, have headquarters or branches in Madrid. The city's broad avenues are lined with modern office buildings and government centers.

Modern Madrid is quite different from the sleepy little town King Philip II found when he moved his capital there in 1561. King Philip thought that Madrid's location in the center of the nation would help unify Spain. Another king, Ferdinand VII, founded Madrid's Prado Museum. Today, the Prado is one of the greatest art museums in the world. Still another king, Juan Carlos I, now lives in Madrid in the Royal Palace. The palace is one of the most amazing buildings in the world. It has 2,800 rooms and is surrounded by a stately, formal garden.

A short drive away from Madrid is Ávila in Old Castile. Although Ávila has thriving wool and tanning (leather) industries, it is more famous for its historic sites. Ávila was built in the Middle Ages. At that time, it was surrounded by a thick stone wall to protect its residents from attack. The wall still exists; people who live in Ávila can easily pretend that nine hundred years of history have just rolled away and a knight in shining armor is about to ride through the city.

Citizens of Segovia, a city near Ávila, can imagine they are in an even older era. In Segovia is an ancient aqueduct, which brought water from the mountains.

The Romans built this aqueduct to bring water to the people of Segovia.

This system for transporting water was built by the Romans in the first century A.D. The Romans were such good builders that the stone blocks of the aqueduct stay together without cement or mortar! In the Middle Ages, Segovia was the center of the Spanish textile industry. Today it relies on tourism as a main source of income.

Western and Southern Spain

The region of Estremadura lies in western Spain along the Portuguese border. People in Mérida, a city in Estremadura, also have daily reminders of the Roman era. Every day they drive across a bridge built by Romans two thousand years ago. They may also pass the ruins of a Roman theater and a "circus." The circus was a huge arena seating up to thirty thousand people. Gladiator fights were held there, and at times the circus was flooded to let Roman boats stage sea battles! In spite of its past glory, Estremadura is now one of the poorest areas of Spain. Its soil is poor, and there is little industry.

The South of Spain, Andalusia, has a character all its own. In speaking, Andalusians drop the *th* sound of Castilian; they also omit many other letters and stretch out some sounds. An Andalusian accent is something like some southern accents in the United States—after

The busy port of Málaga in Andalusia is a trading center for wine, fruit, and sugar.

hearing two or three words, you immediately know where the speaker is from!

If you were set down blindfolded in the middle of an Andalusian city, you could also easily guess where you were when you looked around. Andalusian houses have a very special style. They are usually made of white-washed stone. The white paint reflects the strong southern sun, thus keeping the houses cooler. Andalusian houses often have iron balconies filled with flowering plants; many are built around a cool, shady, inner patio.

One of Andalusia's most important industries is tourism. Besides vacationing on the coast, visitors come to see the beautiful buildings constructed by Arabs who lived there from the eighth to the fifteenth centuries. Granada, for example, is the site of the world famous Alhambra Palace. The Alhambra has such delicate designs carved into its stone walls and ceilings that the building appears to be made of lace. In Córdoba, there is a gigantic mosque, or Muslim church, whose roof is supported by 850 columns. When the Arabs were driven out of Spain by Christian rulers, an enormous cathedral was built right inside the mosque! Córdoba and Granada serve as a central market for the rich agricultural products of Andalusia. The cities also have a number of industries, including metal products, cement, chemicals, paper, and food processing.

East and North

Valencia, on Spain's eastern coast, is a region famous for its oranges. Valencia's farmers also produce rice, wheat, corn, and many types of fruit. The soil is very rich in this region, but there is little water. Irrigation is widely used in growing crops here. The people of Valencia are so concerned about the rights to the water in their rivers that a special Water Court has met there

Shepherds tend their flocks in the pastures of the Pyrenees Mountains.

once a week for over a thousand years! There is also a city named Valencia, the third largest in Spain. It contains many beautiful historic sites, including an eight-sided bell tower, *El Miguelete*, which was built in the fourteenth century.

Aragon, one of the least populated areas of Spain, lies along the French border. Sheep are raised in the foothills of the Pyrenees and peaches are grown in the valleys, but there is little industry. However, Aragon is steeped in history—particularly military history. Its capital, Zaragoza, got its name from a blurring of the sounds of "Caesar Augustus," the name of the Roman emperor who was in power when the city was founded. During the nineteenth century, the people of Zaragoza fought off a French army attack that lasted an entire year.

Catalonia and the Basque provinces are two areas in northern Spain that are rich with industry and trade. Barcelona, the traditional capital of Catalonia, is the most important manufacturing city in Spain. The country's second largest city, Barcelona is a major point for trade, since it has an excellent harbor. Manufacturing is also important in Bilbao, in the Basque province. It has great iron and steel-making plants, and is an inland seaport on the Nervión River.

Both the Catalonians and the Basques have their own language, although most people also speak Castilian. For many years, the central government in Madrid outlawed the use of the Catalan and Euskera (Basque) languages, in order to encourage ties with the rest of the country. The government was afraid that these provinces would rebel and break away from Spain to become independent nations. There was some reason for these fears since both areas have always had strong independence movements.

Recently Catalonia and the Basque country have been given much more power to govern themselves. The Catalan and Euskera languages are again permitted and even encouraged. However, some people in these regions still favor complete independence. A few have turned to terrorism to achieve this goal. In the last seventeen years, Basque terrorists have killed about five hundred people in an attempt to further their cause of separation from Spain.

The region of Asturias is ringed by rugged mountains which separate it from the rest of the peninsula. This isolation may have encouraged the fierce independence for which the region is known. During the eighth century, when Moors from Africa swept over the Iberian Peninsula, Asturias was one of the few areas that they could not conquer. Asturias' mountains are the richest coal-mining region in Spain; the area also contains deposits of iron, zinc, lead, and copper. Oviedo, the region's leading city, is an industrial center with many factories producing steel, glass, chemicals, and processed food.

Galicia, in northwestern Spain, also has its own language. Its coastline has many good harbors, and the area supplies one-third of the nation's fish. Almost 30 percent of Spain's cattle are raised in Galicia. However, Galicia has poor soil and little industry, and is another poor area of Spain. During the 1900s, about a million and a half Galicians emigrated to Latin America, the United States, and other parts of Spain.

While praising their own part of Spain, many Spaniards criticize (somewhat jokingly) the rest of the nation. These criticisms often take the form of comments about the reputations of the natives of a particular area. For example, many Spaniards will tell you that a typical Andalusian is happy-go-lucky and somewhat lazy. The word *mañana*, or tomorrow, sums up this view of Andalusians. Mañana means never do anything today that you can possibly put off until tomorrow. Aragonese people are said to have heads so hard and thick—stubborn—that they can hammer nails with them! A typical Galician is often considered poetic, superstitious, and musical; a Castilian is often assumed to be proud. Spaniards sometimes say that Catalonians worship "*Don Dinero*" (Sir Money) and that they could "squeeze bread out of a stone." As for the Basque provinces—well, there's a story about the time the devil hid behind the door of a Basque house because he wanted to learn to speak Euskera. However, after a year of listening the only words he knew were "Yes, ma'am." The story shows how difficult other Spaniards consider Euskera—and how strong they consider Basque women! The language part, at least, is probably true. Not many can pronounce this Basque name: Barrenecheagamechucoicoecheaiturri.

Agriculture and Industry

Although Spain has traditionally been an agricultural country, its farmers have always faced several serious problems. The soil is very poor in most parts of the peninsula, and expensive fertilizers must be used to produce good crops. The land is also very dry, although a network of irrigation canals helps provide water in many areas. Another problem is the lack of modern machinery. In some parts of Spain, grain is still threshed by a mule or an ox pulling a load of stones. In a few areas, water is pumped into the fields by hand or with the help of farm animals. Because of these difficulties, Spanish farmers cannot produce enough food for the entire nation, and Spain must buy what it needs from other countries.

Spain's main cereal crops are wheat and barley. Fruits such as grapes, oranges, lemons, and melons are also grown. The area around Valencia is known for its oranges, rice, and sugar harvests. Andalusia is lined with olive groves; sunflower plants are also grown there, and the seeds are used to make cooking oil. Sheep, goats, and other animals are raised throughout Spain, particularly where the soil is too poor for crops.

In recent years, the number of Spaniards working in industry has increased at a tremendous rate. Many of these are people who can no longer make a living at

Spain is a leading producer of olives.

farming. The government is still trying to encourage the development of new manufacturing and service businesses in Spain. At present, Spain's most important products include cars, ships, steel, cement, chemicals, clothing, and shoes. Fishing is a major source of income in Galicia and the areas that border on the North Atlantic. Tourism is another important nationwide industry. Each year thousands of people flock to "sunny Spain" for vacations.

Developing new industry is important to Spain. This man works in electronics.

Unemployment is a major problem in Spain today. The country lacks many minerals, and its industries must import raw materials. This cuts down on profits and limits the number of workers businesses may hire. Agricultural workers are also affected; there are simply more people available than jobs. To make matters worse, some of the work in farming is seasonal. Many hands are needed at harvest time, but few are employed during the winter months. All of this adds up; in recent years unemployment has risen above 20 percent. This means that one out of every five workers was unable to find a job.

However, in January, 1986, Spain joined the European Community (Common Market), a trading partnership that includes many European countries. Spain's government hopes that this will improve Spain's economy by providing better markets for its exports. The stronger economy should create more jobs for Spanish workers.

Governing the Country

Spain is a parliamentary monarchy. King Juan Carlos I is the head of state and also the commander of the armed forces. The king does not have absolute power, as kings traditionally have; he can propose new laws and approve laws passed by the country's lawmakers. He may declare war and sign peace treaties, and appoint or dismiss high government officials. King Juan Carlos' most important power, however, does not come from the constitution. He is greatly respected by the Spanish people, and because of that he is often able to influence the government's decisions.

The head of the government is the prime minister, who is the leader of the political party that controls

King Juan Carlos I and Queen Sofia, his wife, vote in a national election.

the most seats in Parliament. The prime minister works with a Cabinet to run the government day-to-day. At present, Spain has many political parties, including the Democratic Center Union, the Socialist Workers' Party, the Communist Party, and the Democratic Coalition.

Spain's Parliament, the Cortes, has two houses. The upper house is called the Senate and has 208 members. The Chamber of Deputies, or lower house, has 350 members. Spanish citizens elect representatives to both houses of the Cortes every four years. As does the United States Congress, the Spanish Parliament makes laws, approves treaties, and sets tax rates.

In recent years, Spain has divided itself into seventeen autonomous, or self-governing, regions. Assemblies in each region may pass laws concerning local matters, but may not violate the laws the Cortes has made for the entire country. The powers of the autonomous regions and the central government are balanced much like those of the American states and the federal government in Washington, D.C. The autonomous regions, like Spain as a whole, are democracies. Citizens elect delegates to local and regional assemblies.

As we have seen, the regional assemblies preside over areas with very different geography, customs, and character. Nevertheless, all of Spain's regions also share common bonds, most of them forged during the long history of the peninsula and its people.

2. *The Arts in Spain*

Once upon a time a man lived in the center of Spain in a region called La Mancha. He was of noble birth, but in recent years his family had fallen on hard times and he was now extremely poor. The man was very old and his bones tended to creak when he was active. Therefore, he spent most of his time in the house, reading books about the glorious days of knights and their code of honor called chivalry.

This was a mistake because, by and by, his brain became confused. Although the age of chivalry had ended centuries before, the man began to believe that he was a knight. He found a rusty suit of ancient armor, a broken-down old nag of a horse, and a fat little peasant, Sancho Panza, for a squire. Lastly, he adopted a new name: Don Quixote de la Mancha. Then he rode out into the countryside to save people and fight for justice.

Many of Don Quixote's adventures were comical. For instance, he attacked a windmill, convinced that it was a giant waving its arms. However, Don Quixote wasn't just a clown. His belief in a beautiful, magical world and his idea that one should fight for what is right affected people. Because Don Quixote was a good person, he made everyone around him better, too.

Don Quixote never really lived. He is a character in one of the most famous books in the world, *Don Quixote de la Mancha.* This novel was written in 1605 by Miguel de Cervantes, a writer whose life was almost as exciting as his writing. (Cervantes was wounded in battle, made a slave, captured by pirates, and later arrested after his escape!) Don Quixote does live, though, in the hearts of Spaniards. That's because he shows many of the human qualities most respected in Spain.

First of all, Don Quixote is a true gentleman. He has perfect manners, but his manners are not just on the surface. They come from a deep sense of honor. The Spanish idea of honor means demanding the respect due you, as well as taking full responsibility for your own actions. A professor at the University of Madrid once showed his sense of honor when he arranged an overnight field trip for his students. Because of a mixup in the hotel reservations, there were not enough rooms for everyone. Although he was nearly eighty, the professor insisted on giving up his room to a student. He spent the night on the bus. "A gentleman cannot rest when those he is responsible for are uncomfortable," he explained.

Don Quixote is also an idealist; he believes that a perfect world is possible, and he often tries to achieve what everyone else considers impossible. Many scholars have observed this same habit in Spanish history—in the 1930s constitution, for example, which tried to reform every aspect of Spanish life. The effort failed, but it was a courageous try.

Macho Man

Don Juan is another important, but imaginary, figure in Spain. Don Juan is a character in many of the world's great plays, poems, and operas. He was created in the seventeenth century by a Spanish playwright named Tirso de Molina. Don Juan is a handsome man who attracts the attention of women wherever he goes. However, he is also heartless. His habit is to win a girl's love and then abandon her after a few days. In Tirso de Molina's version, Don Juan pays dearly for this behavior. He challenges the statue of a dead man to a duel and dies when the ghost returns to fight him. At the end of the play, the ghost takes Don Juan to eternal punishment.

A few centuries later, José Zorilla was kinder to Don Juan in the play he wrote. Although he is just as evil in this version, Don Juan is loved by a very saintly woman. Her prayers are enough to save him. Don Juan has a change of heart and ascends to heaven with her when he dies. Because of its hopeful ending, this play is often performed on All Souls' Day, November 2, the feast day on which Catholics pray for the souls of the dead.

Like Don Quixote, Don Juan is popular because he expresses some ideas that are widely accepted in Spain. Although no one believes that abandoning women is the right thing to do, many Spaniards admire Don Juan's manliness. Besides being attractive, Don Juan is strong and clearly in charge where women are concerned. These qualities are summed up with one word: *macho.* A macho or "manly" man doesn't help with the dishes; that's women's work. He whistles or whispers compliments when he passes a pretty woman on the street. He alone decides what is best for his family, and he expects his wife to go along with his ideas.

Until recently, that's just what almost all Spanish wives did! Traditionally, Spanish women led very sheltered lives. They were expected to remain in the home, cooking, cleaning, and caring for their husbands and children. Few women held outside jobs, except when the income was absolutely necessary for the family. As the men respected Don Juan, many women looked up to the saintly woman who saved him. They admired her holiness and her willingness to devote herself to the man she loved.

In recent years, many Spanish women have begun to seek more equality. A women's liberation movement has been organized, and women have pressed for better jobs and salaries. Although there are still many traditional macho men in Spain, women have made some gains. A small number have founded their own businesses or reached the top positions in established companies. There are more women in professions such as law and medicine, and a woman was recently appointed to one of the highest governing councils in Spain.

In the home, some Spanish women are also achieving greater equality. Some now expect their husbands to do their share of the housework and childrearing, and consider themselves full partners in the family's decisions. However, most Spanish families still follow the more traditional roles.

A Streak of Sadness

Federico García Lorca, another famous Spanish writer, also captured part of his nation's soul in his writing. García Lorca was born in Granada in 1898. He often wrote poems about the South of Spain, and much of his writing is very sad. In one of his poems, for example, he speaks of the city of Córdoba as "far away and alone." A rider is traveling to Córdoba on a black horse, but Death is watching, and the rider knows he will never get there. Federico García Lorca may have had a feeling about his own future when he wrote that poem. A few months later, during the Spanish Civil War, he was shot while in prison.

Although Spaniards love parties and can be very merry, the sadness of García Lorca's poem is also a part of their character—perhaps because life on the Iberian Peninsula has never been easy. The harsh climate, the poverty, and the wars in Spain's history have given Spaniards reason to mourn.

This sadness is also reflected in Spain's most famous music, *flamenco.* Flamenco music is played on a guitar and is accompanied by singing, hand-clapping, and foot-stamping. Dancers whirl to flamenco music, clicking little wooden shells called castanets and tapping out the dance's rhythm with sturdy shoes. Although the beat appears lively, most flamenco songs are about lost love, poverty, and unhappiness. One type of flamenco music is the *solea.* A typical solea describes a poor family working long hours in the fields. Although they dream of buying their own farm one day, they know they will never achieve their goal.

Of course, not all Spanish music is sad; *zarzuelas* are actually joyous! Zarzuelas are plays set to music. The actors sing and dance throughout the performance and occasionally speak a few lines of dialogue. The stories are usually funny and romantic.

In addition to flamenco and the zarzuela, each region of Spain also has its own folk music. In Galicia,

These women are dancing the fandango*, a popular Spanish folk dance.*

where the Celts from Ireland invaded long ago, musicians often play the bagpipe, and dancers' steps resemble the Irish jig. In Aragon, the *jota* has long been popular, and in Catalonia, people traditionally have danced the *sardana.* These dances are often held outside. In Barcelona on Sunday mornings, the main plaza fills with hundreds of dancers and musicians. The dancers join hands and move gracefully to a slow beat.

One custom popular in all the provinces of Spain is the *tuna.* A tuna is a small singing group of young men, usually from the same university. Members of the tuna wear clothes patterned after sixteenth-century styles: short, full pants; black stockings; short jackets; and long, full capes. The tuna traditionally serenades pretty girls. The singers stand in the street as the young lady sits on her balcony. When the songs are finished, the girl throws colorful ribbons to the musicians. The tuna members pin the ribbons onto their capes. They often have whole rainbows of ribbons on their clothing!

Spain can also boast of some musicians who are famous all over the world. Andrés Segovia is probably the best guitar player ever. He invented a method for playing classical pieces on the guitar that created a whole new type of music. Although over ninety, Segovia was still touring Europe and the Americas in the 1980s, giving sold-out concerts in many cities. Alicia de Larrocha, who plays classical music on the piano, also performs internationally. Placido Domingo, Victoria de los Angeles, and Montserrat Caballe are world-famous opera singers.

The Art of Spain

If you travel on Spain's national airline, Iberia, it's possible to fly on a jet named "El Greco." El Greco was a

Members of a tuna stroll through the streets, stopping to serenade a young lady.

master painter who worked in Spain in the sixteenth century. (His name means "the Greek," which is where he was born. Domenikos Theotokopoulos, his actual name, was too hard for Spaniards to pronounce! Nevertheless, he lived most of his life in Spain and is considered a Spanish painter.) The fact that the airline chose to name one of its planes after an artist shows how much Spaniards have always respected art.

El Greco's paintings have a very unusual style. They often show people with long, sad faces, and they are painted in unreal colors with many patches of shadow and light. Diego Velázquez, on the other hand, painted more realistically. He lived in the seventeenth century and was the official court painter for King Philip IV. One of his most famous pictures shows the tiny princess Margarita Teresa and her maids of honor. The dwarf who entertained the royalty at court, the princess' pet dog, the king and queen, and even Velázquez himself are also in the picture.

Another great Spanish artist, Francisco Goya, was born in 1746. Goya also painted portraits of royalty, but he was not always kind to his subjects. If Goya did not like the king or queen, he painted every wrinkle and ugly feature, exactly as he saw it. Goya is also famous for a series of drawings called "The Disasters of War," which show terrible scenes of suffering and death during a Spanish revolution.

Pablo Picasso was a pioneer in modern art. His painting Three Musicians *(1921) is an example of Cubism.*

A more recent Spanish master, Pablo Picasso, also criticized violence by means of his art. Picasso was born in Málaga in 1881. He was one of the first painters to produce Cubist art—a style in which shapes like squares, circles, and triangles are used to represent people and objects. Although Picasso spent much of his adult life in France, he often used Spanish themes in his

This street artist carries on Spain's rich creative tradition.

work. One of his most famous drawings, for example, is of Don Quixote and his helper Sancho Panza. Another canvas, "Guernica," shows a Spanish tragedy. During the Spanish Civil War, after German bombers destroyed the Basque city of Guernica, Picasso created the huge painting to show the agony caused by the bombing. In "Guernica," a mother holds her dead baby. Her whole head is shaped like a screaming mouth and her eyes have turned into tears.

Pablo Picasso died in 1973, but the tradition of Spanish art continues. Some art experts estimate that there are about five hundred internationally known Spanish artists working today. One of these is Antonio López García, who paints and sculpts wood. López García is a patient man—one of his pictures of Madrid took eight years to create, and another took twenty years! Another current artist, Miguel Barceló, creates pictures with paint and such objects as string, paper strips, and cigarette butts.

Today, Spain has about 2,500 art galleries which often feature the work of new and unknown artists as well as the pictures painted by well-known artists. That's a huge number of galleries for such a small country! Along with many Spanish writers, dancers, and musicians, Spain's painters share their nation's love of self-expression, and continue its rich creative tradition.

3. *Spain's Changing Face*

Over thirteen thousand years ago, one of the world's first artists entered a cave deep inside a hill in northern Spain. The artist lay down on a broad, flat stone close to the roof of the cave. Within easy reach were several sea shells to use as drawing tools, each containing a different color. "Paint" was made of dark brown, tan, and reddish bits of dirt or charcoal mixed with grease and cork. With strong, sure strokes, the artist sketched a number of animals on the white limestone ceiling and walls of the cave—bulls, deer, bear, and wild boar.

Many years passed, and the artist's people died or moved away. Natural forces in the earth changed the shape of the land. Huge boulders closed off the entrance to the cave. Air and moisture, which might have damaged the paintings, were nearly sealed out.

The drawings were in almost perfect condition in 1879, when a young Spanish girl named Maria de Santuola found a crack in the rock and looked through it. At home, she told her father about the marvelous pictures she had seen inside Altamira cave. Although we can only make guesses about who drew the pictures, and why, Altamira became famous throughout the world as one of the best examples of prehistoric art.

Prehistoric peoples built structures like this dolmen, which may have been used as a tomb.

The Altamira pictures are extremely old, but even so, they are not the work of the earliest Spaniards. Historians believe that human beings first arrived on the Iberian Peninsula over 100,000 years ago. Little remains from that long period of unrecorded history. Besides Altamira and other painted caves, scientists have also found some stone tools and a number of dolmens.

Dolmens are small buildings made of slabs of rock. They were probably used as tombs.

These prehistoric tribes, however, are not the only ancestors of present-day Spaniards. Time after time, Spain has experienced waves of immigration and invasion from other countries. The Iberians walked into the country from northern Africa around 3000 B.C. At that time, Europe and Africa were connected by a land bridge that later became submerged and turned into the Strait of Gibraltar. The Iberians gave their name to the peninsula. They settled along the Ebro River. (Ebro comes from the Iberian word *iber*, which means "river.") These people built Spain's first cities, and two of their settlements, Tarragona and Cartagena, are still in existence today.

The Iberians were fierce fighters who erected strong walls around their cities to protect themselves. Their artists decorated vases with pictures of warriors fighting on foot, on horseback, and from the decks of small boats. The Iberians also crafted delicate gold pins, bracelets, and necklaces. They created many bronze statues of bulls, other animals, and flowers. The most famous remaining artwork of the Iberians is a stone statue of a young woman. Since she was found near the town of Elche, she is called "The Lady of Elche." The "Lady" wears many pieces of jewelry and a huge headdress, and may have been an Iberian princess.

Around 1200 B.C. another people, the Phoenicians, arrived in Spain. The Phoenicians came from the Middle East. Although they founded the cities of Cádiz and Málaga, the Phoenicians were not really interested in maintaining colonies in Spain. They were a trading nation, and they wanted the silver, gold, copper, lead, and other minerals of western Spain.

Another wave of people entered Spain in 900 B.C., and again in 600 B.C. These immigrants were the Celts, the same ethnic group that populated Ireland, Scotland, and Wales. The Celts settled in northern Spain. As they spread southward, the Celts often found themselves at war with the Iberians. However, in time the Celts and the Iberians intermarried and formed a new group, the Celtiberians. Around 600 B.C. the ancient Greeks traveled to Spain to trade with the Celtiberians. The Greeks established a number of settlements, but like the Phoenicians, they were not interested in forming more colonies.

The inhabitants of Carthage, on the other hand, did conquer large sections of Spain. Carthage was a Phoenician city in North Africa located near the site of today's Tunis, Tunisia. Around 300 B.C. Hamilcar Barca, a Carthaginian leader, founded Barcelona. Barca's son Hannibal conquered all of Spain south of the Ebro River. Hannibal also attempted to defeat the mighty Roman Empire and is remembered for using elephants in his war on Rome. Although he won some important battles, in the end Hannibal was not successful. In fact, Roman troops attacked Carthaginian armies in Spain and eventually drove the Carthaginians off the Iberian Peninsula entirely.

The Roman Era

Roman soldiers fought the Carthaginians and native Spanish tribes for control of Spain for almost two hundred years. Because of their fierce courage, the Spaniards became famous throughout the empire. In fact, one whole legion of Roman troops revolted when they found out they were being sent to fight in Spain! Once the war was over, however, the people of Iberia settled down to a long period of peace. Spain became Hispania, a Roman province.

The Romans made many contributions to Spain during the almost four centuries they ruled there. They founded or enlarged eight hundred cities and crisscrossed the province with roads. They built theaters, bridges, arenas, and aqueducts to carry water. The Romans also introduced Christianity to Hispania in the first century A.D. By 325, almost everyone in Spain was a member of that faith. The Roman language, Latin, also spread throughout the land. (Today, four of the five main languages of the Iberian Peninsula—Spanish,

Romans constructed many buildings like this theater at Mérida during their rule.

Portuguese, Galician, and Catalan—are based on Latin.) The common language and religion, as well as the strong Roman government, changed the small separate tribes of the peninsula into a united group.

In return, Hispania supplied Rome with minerals, livestock, and food crops. At one point, Hispania was the wealthiest province of the entire empire. Three

Roman emperors, Trajan, Hadrian, and Theodosius, were born there. Several famous Roman authors, including Seneca, Lucan, and Martial, also came from Hispania.

When the Roman Empire crumbled in the fifth century, the same Germanic tribes that overran Italy invaded the Iberian Peninsula as well. One of these tribes, the Visigoths, conquered all of Hispania in 573. The Visigoths greatly admired the Romans whose empire they had helped to destroy. Their nobles soon adopted Spanish customs, language, and religion. However, the Visigoths proved to be poor governors; during their reign the strong central government of the Roman era began to break down, and the country split into tiny kingdoms. At one point, there were more than thirty Visigothic kings in Spain, most of whom were squabbling with their neighbors!

The Moors

Because of this weakness, it was relatively easy for Sheik Tarik Aben Zyad (the One-Eyed) to lead an army of Moors from Morocco in North Africa to Spain in 711. His landing place was named "Tarik's Rock" in his honor. (In Arabic this is *jebel Tarik*, which eventually became "Gibraltar.") Tarik was followed by thousands of other Arabs. By 718, all of the Iberian Peninsula,

The Moors ruled Spain for nearly 800 years. These men are dressed in Moorish clothing.

except for a small strip of land across the northern coast, was controlled by Arabs.

The Arabs were Muslims, or followers of the religion of Islam. Although they had conquered Spain in honor of their God, Allah, they allowed the native Spaniards to practice their own religions. In the seven hundred years that they were in Spain, the Moors made many contributions to Spanish culture. They constructed hundreds of beautiful palaces, castles, and mosques. Arab scholars also brought advanced knowledge of medicine, astronomy, and mathematics to Spain. One Arab ruler, Abd-al-Rahman I, introduced new farming methods into southern Spain. With the help of irrigation, Spanish farmers began to grow banana trees, sugar cane, cotton, and date palms during his reign. Abd-al-Rahman also promoted silk weaving, paper making, and leather crafts. His artisans became skilled in a type of elaborate metal decoration called damascene work, which is still done in Spain today.

The Reconquest

Although the Arabs remained in Spain until the fifteenth century, their control of the peninsula was often challenged. The native Spaniards revolted frequently. One important battle occurred in 722. In that year, a Spanish chieftain named Pelayo gathered his

The Moors built many fortified palaces called alcázares, like this one in Segovia.

followers in a cave called Covadonga in northern Spain. The Arab army sent to defeat Pelayo failed. Even so, the Arab rulers did not consider Pelayo important enough to challenge with another attack. No harm could come from such a small band of warriors, they reasoned.

They were wrong. Through the years, Pelayo became a symbol of Spanish resistance, and his kingdom, Asturias, became the starting point of the Spanish rebellion against their Arab conquerors. The period of time between the battle of Covadonga and the final defeat of the Moors in 1492 is called "the Reconquest" by Spanish historians. During this seven-hundred-year period, native Spaniards won back their lands piece by tiny piece. As each area came under Spanish control again, the conquerors formed new kingdoms. These Christian kingdoms, eager to expand their power, often went to war with each other. In addition, the Arab states of Spain often quarrelled among themselves. So the inhabitants of Spain saw every form of war during the long period of Arab rule—Spaniard against Arab, Spaniard against Spaniard, and Arab against Arab.

Pelayo was not the only hero of the Reconquest. Rodrigo Díaz de Vivar, who lived in the eleventh century, was a subject of the king of Castile. He was expelled from Castile for his opposition to the hated king. Díaz de Vivar raised an army and hired himself and his soldiers to various rulers. He defeated an Arab army from Granada to earn the title *El Cid Campeador*, which means "lord winner of battles." El Cid, as he became known, fought many other wars for several different leaders, both Spanish and Arab. He became very wealthy and powerful, and eventually took Valencia back from the Moors in 1094. One of the earliest works of Spanish literature, "The Poem of El Cid," was written about his adventures. Although most of the poem concentrates on El Cid's heroism, he also comes across as a real human being. In one verse, his parting from his wife, Ximena, is described as "a fingernail parting from the skin" because it was so painful. In another verse, El Cid pulls the beard of a nobleman who insulted him!

Ferdinand and Isabella

When the Arabs' last stronghold, Granada, was taken back in 1492, the conquering armies belonged to Queen Isabella of Castile and King Ferdinand of Aragon. These Spanish rulers had married in 1469, uniting their two kingdoms. Isabella, an extremely intelligent woman, was raised to believe that nothing was more important than religion. Ferdinand was a courageous soldier. He and Isabella followed their armies from battle to battle; several of the couple's ten children were born in military camps. Ferdinand and Isabella ruled

Spain as powerful partners. In fact, their royal motto was "Isabella is the equal of Ferdinand."

To Ferdinand and Isabella, the effort to drive the Moors from Spain was a religious crusade. They wanted all of their subjects to follow the Catholic faith. To achieve this goal, Ferdinand and Isabella also established the Inquisition in 1480. It was to operate for about three hundred years. The Inquisition was a religious court with unlimited power to imprison, torture, and kill anyone suspected of not believing in Catholic teachings. Protestants, Jews, and Muslims were often arrested. Catholics whose faith seemed different from the established religion were also tried by the Inquisition. Those convicted of heresy were usually given three choices: to change religions, to die, or to leave Spain. Over two thousand Spaniards, most of them innocent, were executed by the Inquisition. About 150,000 people fled from it to other European or African countries.

The Inquisition also banned books it considered dangerous to the Catholic faith. To find these books, a simple test was used. The Inquisition believed that books which were truly holy would not burn. So texts accused of being anti-religious were thrown into a fire. Needless to say, this test proved the Inquisition's suspicions correct again and again.

Though today people view the Inquisition as shameful, the reign of Ferdinand and Isabella was also marked by great achievements. In 1492 Isabella agreed to finance an expedition to find a water route to Asia. The captain, Christopher Columbus, never reached the Far East. However, the New World he found more than made up for this failure!

The Spanish Empire

During the fifteenth and sixteenth centuries, many Spanish explorers were drawn to the Americas. Vasco Núñez de Balboa led an expedition across Panama and became the first European to see the eastern shore of the Pacific Ocean. Hernando Cortés conquered the mighty Aztec Empire of Mexico, and Francisco Pizarro claimed Peru, where the Inca people lived, for Spain. Juan Ponce de León explored the present state of Florida; Hernando De Soto, Alvar Núñez Cabeza de Vaca, and Francisco de Coronado were the first Europeans to travel through what is now the southern United States.

These *conquistadores*, or "conquerors," claimed vast amounts of land for Spain. Of course, all of this territory was home to the native North and South American Indians. In the Spaniards' view, claiming the Indians' land and possessions was not stealing, and even killing or enslaving them was acceptable.

At the same time, Spanish conquistadores invaded and won territory in North Africa and parts of Europe.

The conquistador Hernando Cortés conquered much of central and southern Mexico, including the Aztec Empire.

Soon a vast Spanish Empire was formed. At its height, the empire included Mexico, California, the American Southwest, half of South America, Portugal, and parts of North Africa, France, Italy, Belgium, and the Netherlands. The last two areas had been ruled by a grandson of Ferdinand and Isabella, Charles I. Charles was a Hapsburg, a member of the royal family that was to rule Spain for almost two hundred years.

This huge empire brought Spain tremendous wealth. Gold, silver, and other treasures from the Americas poured into Spain. The nation seemed to be riding a wave of success. Even Spanish artists and writers felt the effects; the sixteenth and seventeenth centuries are known as Spain's "Golden Age" because of the great literature and art produced during this period.

However, even as the wave of success reached its crest, situations which would eventually destroy the empire were developing. First of all, conquering other countries is very costly. Each war drained Spain of men and money. Many Spanish colonies also revolted against their rulers, resulting in more wars, more lost lives, and more expense. In addition, the government made a number of extremely unwise laws. Each Spanish shoemaker, for example, was allowed to make only certain styles of shoes. This limited customers to people who were not bored with those particular models. Also, wealth from the colonies did not reach the common people of Spain. The country had a huge group of poor peasants and a small, tremendously rich ruling class. Not surprisingly, many Spaniards decided to leave their homeland to seek their fortunes in the New World. Since many Jews and Moriscos (Arabs who had converted to the Catholic religion) had already been expelled by the Inquisition, Spain had a shortage of workers, and the economy suffered.

The year 1588 marked the beginning of the end of the Spanish Empire. In that year, King Philip II decided to send a mighty force of Spanish ships to fight England. The fleet was called the Armada, and Philip expected an easy victory over the British. Instead, poor weather, lack of supplies, and unwise military decisions brought defeat to Spain. After 1588 the empire lost territory in a series of wars. By the late seventeenth century, many of Spain's conquered European lands were gone. France even controlled parts of Spain itself. When the Spanish King Charles II died without an heir, a Frenchman, Philip of Anjou, took the throne as Philip V. This touched off yet another long and costly war among several European nations. This "War of Spanish Succession" ended in 1714. All the rest of Spain's possessions in Europe were taken away. Philip V was allowed to keep his throne; the line of kings he began was called the Bourbons.

The Bourbons ruled for about a hundred years.

Then in 1808 Napoleon Bonaparte, the French emperor, seized control of Spain's government and put his brother on the throne of Spain. Joseph Bonaparte was hated by the Spaniards. People called him *Pepe Botellas* ("Joe Bottles") because they considered him a drunkard. The discontented Spaniards drove Napoleon out after five years of hit-and-run, guerrilla warfare. The Spanish kings returned to the throne, but they were not to remain there for long.

Early in the nineteenth century, Spaniards who wanted more rights for the people and a limit to royal power wrote a constitution. However, their rulers would not allow it to be put into effect. Throughout the century, there were constant quarrels between supporters of the constitution and supporters of the monarchy. To make matters worse, those who favored a royal government also disagreed among themselves. When Ferdinand VII died in 1833, some Spaniards wanted his daughter Isabella to rule. Others, who were called Carlists, supported Ferdinand's eldest brother, Carlos. Isabella became queen, but the Carlists were never satisfied with her.

In the last years of the nineteenth century, there was great unrest in Spain. Spain's last foreign colonies, Cuba and the Philippines, were taken away after the Spanish-American War of 1898, a five-month war with the United States. The military revolted, the monarchy was exiled and returned, and a republic was established for a brief period. (In a republic, laws are made by representatives of the people.) In 1923 an army general named Miguel Primo de Rivera led a revolution. King Alfonso XIII, knowing he had no real choice, supported the revolution. Primo de Rivera became prime minister, but he had the powers of a dictator. He ruled until 1930, when the army overthrew the government. Finally, in 1931 general elections were held in Spain. The people voted overwhelmingly in favor of a republic. Alfonso XIII fled the country, and there was great rejoicing throughout Spain. "We have had a revolution without spilling a single drop of blood!" the people exclaimed.

The Republic and Civil War

These words came back to haunt Spain only a few years later, for the Republic was doomed to fail. Everyone who supported the Republic agreed that conditions in Spain had to change. Unfortunately, that was the only thing they agreed on. Land reform was needed, for instance. The Republic passed a law breaking up some huge estates so that land could be distributed to the peasants. The law was immediately attacked—both by those who thought it was too strong and by those who thought it was too weak. Each side formed a political party and tried to gain power in the government. Spain ended up with too many political parties, all fighting each other, each gaining and losing power almost daily. In four-and-a-half years of republican government, Spain had twenty-six major political crises and seventy-two different ministers in its government.

The Republic also tried to accomplish more than was possible. It once passed a law requiring that all Spanish children attend school. However, when the law was passed there were only enough schools to accept one quarter of the nation's students!

Another explosive issue was the role of the Catholic church in Spain. Since the days of the Inquisition, the Catholic religion had been almost the only faith in Spain. The church owned huge amounts of land and was closely tied to the ruling classes. When the Republic began its reforms, it often clashed with the church. Some angry radicals who supported these reforms attacked priests and nuns and burned church property. This upset many sincerely religious Spaniards and made them enemies of the Republic.

In July, 1936, three English tourists landed in the Canary Islands. They had come to Spain in a small, private plane. The next day, officials at the airfield were surprised to see that the plane was gone. The tourists were stranded. Though they pretended to be surprised, the "tourists" had really expected this to happen. They were actually part of a plot to smuggle General Francisco Franco into Morocco to lead a rebellion against the Spanish Republic.

Franco was born in the city of El Ferrol, Galicia, in 1892. He attended a military academy in Toledo, and then rose quickly in the Spanish army. Serving for many years in Morocco, he was a respected leader. In 1936 he became Chief of Staff of the army of the Spanish Republic. However, he soon found he disagreed with the policies of the government. In the spring of 1936, he was ordered to the Canary Islands. When he secretly left the Canary Islands for Morocco, he committed an act of treason. But he would go further yet—he would return to the mainland from Morocco to begin the Spanish Civil War.

The Spanish Civil War was one of the bloodiest wars in history. On one side were Franco, other army officers, the church, and all those who believed in a government ruled by a single, strong person. They were known as Nationalists. Franco's forces received troops, money, planes, and weapons from the dictators of Italy and Germany, Benito Mussolini and Adolf Hitler. On the other side were the Republicans and an assortment of political parties that wanted more power for individual Spaniards. They were aided by Russia, and by thousands of people around the world who viewed the Spanish Civil War as a struggle for democracy. Some

Generalíssimo Francisco Franco led the Nationalist Army during the Spanish Civil War. In this 1936 photograph, he reviews some of his troops.

Republican supporters sent money and supplies. Others actually came to Spain to fight. A large group calling itself the Abraham Lincoln Brigade arrived from America.

The war was fought from town to town for three long years, until General Franco triumphed in 1939. At the end of the Civil War, over 640,000 Spaniards were dead; 400,000 were in exile; and 2,000,000 were in jail. Spain had suffered over twelve billion dollars worth of damage. Just about every family in Spain had lost a relative, friend, or home to the war.

The Franco Years

During the war, General Franco took the title of *Generalíssimo* or "supreme commander." In 1939 the Generalíssimo organized what he called a "temporary" government to bring the country back to normal. This temporary government lasted almost forty years, until Franco's death in 1975.

Spaniards who lived through the Franco years are divided in their opinion of him. Many older people who remember the horrors of the Civil War praise the Generalíssimo for bringing the country such a long period of peace. They also credit Franco with the improvement in living conditions. Although Spain has never been a rich country, Spain had one of the highest rates of economic growth in the world during the 1950s and 1960s. Businesses started and expanded at a fast pace. Under the Franco government, there were also many improvements in education, medical care, and transportation. Some Spaniards even jokingly referred to their leader as "Froggy Franco" because he opened so many new water projects to help the farmers.

However, younger Spaniards often point out that the benefits of Franco's rule carried a high price tag. "Generalíssimo" was really another name for dictator. Franco was the supreme ruler of the country. Though the Spanish Cortes continued to meet, it had no real power. Furthermore, representatives could only be members of one political party—Franco's. All other political parties were banned, as were trade unions, demonstrations, and newspapers that criticized the government.

Franco also chose his successor. Juan Carlos I, the Bourbon grandson of Alfonso XIII, grew up at Franco's side. Franco spent a great deal of time with the young prince, teaching him how to carry on the same type of government after Franco's death. When Franco died, many Spaniards doubted that the new king would be strong enough to hold the country together. They thought that Franco's death would trigger another civil war, and referred to the king as "Juan Carlos the Brief."

Instead, the impossible happened. King Juan Carlos proved to be a good leader, able to listen to all sides but strong in his own beliefs. Surprisingly, his ideas were very different from Franco's. Only five days after taking power, he granted a pardon to political prisoners. A short while later, he allowed free trade unions to form and lifted the ban on political parties. In 1977 Spain had its first free election since the days of the Republic. In his first speech to the new Cortes, Juan Carlos announced, "Democracy has begun." Four years later, when civil guards and the army attempted a military takeover, Juan Carlos went on television to plead for the rights of Spaniards to have a voice in their government. He said democracy would be destroyed "over [his] dead body." Because of the king's influence, the revolt failed.

Spain changed greatly during the first decade of Juan Carlos' reign. Besides becoming a democracy, the country also strengthened its ties with other European countries. Spain became a member of NATO (the North Atlantic Treaty Organization), a defense organization that includes the United States and many European countries. In January, 1986, Spain was admitted to the European Community, a trade group of European nations. Spain went a long way towards ending its traditional isolation during the 1980s. Foreign movies, books, and art exhibits are now common in Spain; during the Franco years many of these cultural exchanges were banned by the government.

Spain also broke some of its traditional ties with the Catholic church. Divorce, birth control, and some abortions (activities opposed by the church) were made legal. Censorship was also abolished. For the first time in decades, Spaniards are allowed to question their government's policies. A number of new magazines and newspapers containing lively debates on political and social problems have been established.

Not every change has been welcomed. Some people believe that the new freedom has led to the breakdown of traditional Spanish values. These people point to a rising crime rate and a huge increase in pornography as two problems of modern Spain. Others feel that new customs from America and other countries are overshadowing Spain's own culture. Video games and cassette players, for example, have encouraged more people to stay at home in the evenings—a time most Spaniards traditionally spent taking a walk or chatting in a café.

Still, Spain looks to the future. In 1986 Juan Carlos' son Felipe (Philip) was named "Prince of Asturias." According to Spanish custom, this title is given to the successor to the Spanish throne, in honor of Pelayo, the Asturian chief who began the Reconquest in 722. Although Felipe is young, most Spaniards admire him and look forward to his reign. However, it seems certain that democracy is now firmly established in Spain. The future King Felipe will be a limited monarch, much as Queen Elizabeth II is in Britain. He will be the most famous person in the next generation of Spaniards—a people whose history stretches back through the Civil War, the age of Columbus, the Roman Empire, and the coming of the Iberians, to the unknown artist who sketched a bull on the ceiling of Altamira cave.

4. The Arabe Duck and Other Tales

When the Moors invaded Spain, a little duck came with them. This animal, whose name was Arabe Duck, was very hungry. However, he was also lazy and he did not like to hunt for his food like other animals. So Arabe Duck went to the shore of a pond and said to an old crab who was resting there, "I can tell the future by looking at the stars. This pond will dry up soon. Gather all the fish for me, and I will carry them in my beak to another pond." Of course, Arabe Duck intended to eat the fish, not save them.

The crab was rather stupid, so he did what Arabe Duck wanted. But crabs have eyes in the backs of their heads. When the crab headed into the water, Arabe Duck thought the crab couldn't see him, but he was wrong. The crab saw the fish disappearing down Arabe Duck's throat.

The crab came back to Arabe Duck and said, "Bend your head, little duck, and I will hold it with my claw. Then you can carry me to another pond, too." Arabe Duck bent down, and the powerful claws of the crab caught him. That was the end of Arabe Duck!

Spanish children often hear the story of Arabe Duck while they are growing up. Arabe Duck is typical

(Next two pages) *The Alhambra, built by the Moors, is said to house the ghosts of many warriors.*
(Inset) *According to Spanish stories, ghosts may walk this courtyard in the Alhambra when the moon is full.*

of many Spanish folktales because the story shows an Arab in a bad light. It seems that Spaniards, at least in their folktales, have not forgiven the Moors for invading Spain centuries ago!

Even so, Spaniards continue to be fascinated by their enemies of long ago. Another story, "The Golden Pitcher," tells of a long-dead Moorish princess whose spirit is not allowed to rest. During her lifetime she had become a Christian, and her family had placed a curse on her. She was condemned to haunt a cave until a pure, kind Spanish girl agreed to hold her hand and pass through the trials of hell with her. Conchita, a poor peasant girl, finally helped the poor princess, and received a golden pitcher as a reward.

The Spaniards also tell tales of Moorish ghosts who sleep in the Alhambra, their former palace in Granada. According to the stories, the ghosts of many warriors and of the last Arab king, Boabdil, wait for the day when they will awaken and reclaim Granada. Until that time, they may break their rest only when the moon is full. On those nights, they walk the courtyard of their ancient palace.

To Zaragoza or Back to the Pond

Some Spanish fairy tales poke fun at people from various regions in Spain. Aragonese, for example, have a reputation throughout Spain as being stubborn. In one old tale, an Aragonese man is journeying to Zaragoza. He can see the city just a short way off when another traveler asks him where he is going. "To Zaragoza," he replies. The traveler reminds him to add, "If God wills it," but the Aragonese insists that he will go "whether God wills it or not." The traveler, who is a saint in disguise, then changes the Aragonese into a frog and places him in a small pond. A year later he returns and asks the frog where he is going. The stubborn Aragonese still replies, "To Zaragoza!" and lands back in the pond. Every year the saint returns and asks again; every year the Aragonese is too thick-headed to change his answer!

Because Spain is a Catholic nation, many of its legends deal with saints. Since the Middle Ages, Spaniards have told a story about Saint James of Zebedee, one of Jesus' twelve apostles. The legend says that St. James, who is called Santiago in Spanish, once preached in Galicia. He loved the land so much that after his death his followers sent his body back there. A stone opened magically to receive the body, and the land of the province, which had been dry and harsh, became the most fertile in Spain. The rock moved magically many times, and then came to rest at Compostela, where a great cathedral was built. Pilgrims were said to be guided to the spot by a path of stars.

Few Spaniards today believe the legend of St. James, though the Milky Way is still called "the Way of Santiago" in Spanish. However, centuries ago people from all over Europe made pilgrimages to Compostela to pray to St. James. They wore small sea shells on their clothes in honor of the saint because, according to another legend, Santiago once saved a pilgrim from drowning in the sea.

Many Spanish fairy tales are just for fun. Children hear lots of stories about Ratón Pérez (Perez the Mouse) and his friend Hormiguita (Little Ant) while they are growing up. They also know about the Carlanco, a monster who is similar to America's Big Bad Wolf. In one tale, the Carlanco tries to capture three young goats. Their mother had locked them in the house when she went out, telling them not to open the door for anyone but her. When the Carlanco knocks, the little goats refuse to answer. However, the monster waits nearby until the mother goat returns. He hears her say, "Open the door, my daughters three; here is your mother, so open for me."

The next day when the mother leaves, the Carlanco again tries to enter the house. He says exactly what the mother had said the day before. The little goats open the door, but they run into the attic when they see the Carlanco rushing in. The mother goat returns to find her door locked, a raging monster in her living room,

During the Middle Ages, as many as two million people a year made pilgrimages to the magnificent cathedral of Santiago de Compostela.

and her crying children in the attic! Luckily, the mother goat had once done a favor for a wasp. The wasp flies through the window and stings the Carlanco many times. The monster runs out of the house in pain and fright, and the goats are saved.

Coplas and Riddles

Animals appear in *coplas* too—but then, just about everything appears in Spanish coplas! Coplas are short poems set to music. The oldest coplas were written centuries ago; the newest ones are being written right now, by any Spaniard who feels like making up a song. Mothers sing them as lullabies. Drivers make them up to pass time on the road. Workers sing them together, and farmers hum them in the fields. As one copla says:

I have a little jug
Of coplas and songs.
When I want to enjoy myself
I take the cork away,
and the verses pour out!

Coplas can be funny:

He that loves a woman
Who doesn't love him
Is the same as a bald man
Who finds a comb in the street.

And coplas can be serious:

> What use is it to the prisoner
> To have bars of silver
> And chains of gold
> If he doesn't have freedom?

They can be written about children:

> This tiny baby
> Has no cradle.
> His father is a carpenter
> And will make him one.

And about adults:

> Take, girl, this orange,
> I give it to you because I love you.
> Don't cut it with a knife
> Because my heart is inside.

In other words, coplas can be about anything, by anyone, and sung anytime!

Another popular way to pass the time is to tell riddles. Can you guess the answers to these? (Look at the end of the chapter to see if you are right.)

1. We have two legs, but we can't go anywhere without a man, and he can't go anywhere without us. What are we?

2. What runs and runs and never arrives at its owner's house?

3. As I get bigger, you see less of me. Who am I?

4. A thousand of us travel along one path, but we kick up no dust. Who are we?

5. I live on high, wearing a little golden crown. Even if the Moors come, I cannot run away. Who am I?

Like children all over the world, Spanish boys and girls enjoy telling these riddles to each other. They also love to hear traditional Spanish stories. In recent years, however, the Smurfs, Mickey Mouse, and E.T. have become popular in Spain as well. Little Arabe Duck and the Carlanco have some new, international friends!

(Answers: 1. pants, 2. a windmill, 3. darkness, 4. ants, 5. an acorn)

5. A Year of Holidays

A few minutes before midnight on December 31, people all over Spain make sure they have twelve grapes ready. In Madrid, huge crowds gather in La Puerta del Sol. La Puerta del Sol, which means "Gate of the Sun," is the city center. In other parts of the country, television sets go on. Everyone wants to see—either in person or on TV—the ball that drops at the exact moment the New Year begins. Most important, everyone wants to hear the huge clock of La Puerta del Sol chime the twelve strokes of midnight. At each stroke, Spaniards eat one grape. Swallowing all twelve before the clock stops chiming is said to bring luck during the coming year.

Five nights later, Spain celebrates again. January 6 is the Day of the Three Kings—the feast of Epiphany—which honors the Wise Men who traveled to Bethlehem to bring gifts to the infant Jesus. On the eve of the feast, there are joyous parades. Kings, angels, shepherds, and other figures from the Bible ride through the streets on floats. Little children watch in wonder and try to catch the candy the Kings throw to the crowd.

This probably is not the first time the Spanish children watching such a parade have seen the Wise

Men dressed as the Wise Men ride through the streets on floats as part of the Day of the Three Kings celebration.

Men. For weeks, they have been visiting department stores with their parents to see the Kings. Instead of telling Santa Claus what they want for Christmas, the children tell the Wise Men, and they receive their gifts on the Day of the Three Kings instead of on Christmas morning.

When the parade is over, the children put their shoes on the windowsill, along with a little bit of straw. In the morning, they expect the shoes to be filled with toys. The straw is for the Wise Men's camels to eat!

Holy Week and *Feria*

A few months after the Day of the Three Kings, there is a more serious occasion. During the last week before Easter, Spaniards observe Holy Week. Holy Week reminds people of the death of Christ. In every city and town, there are religious processions. Often in small villages, every single inhabitant joins in a solemn march behind a life-sized cross. A young man dressed as Christ carries the cross. He is guarded by other villagers costumed as Roman soldiers.

Some of the most impressive Holy Week ceremonies are in Seville. Each parish in the city mounts a float carrying a statue of the Virgin Mary. The statues are made of painted wood and are often very old. Parishioners donate jewels and money to make rich robes for each statue. One of the most famous statues is called *La Macarena.* Poor people and bullfighters believe that La Macarena takes care of them, and they often give her special presents.

Although the floats weigh up to a thousand pounds, they are carried by men from each parish. The floats are surrounded by other parishioners dressed in long robes and pointed caps—the same costumes worn by officers of the Inquisition centuries ago. The marchers walk without speaking, because they have taken a vow of silence. From time to time, members of the crowd accompanying them chant a short, sad song called a *saeta.* Saeta comes from the Latin word for "arrow." The songs are "arrows of prayer" shot into heaven.

During Holy Week, just about everyone, even little children, stays up all night long. On Easter Day, everyone is tired. Most Spaniards attend religious services in their parish churches and then spend a quiet day visiting with relatives and friends. A few weeks after Easter, the people of Seville celebrate their city's *Feria.* The Feria is like a three-day party for residents of the city and tourists alike. There are bullfights, circuses, carnivals, and parades of horseback riders. Many families picnic in small, open tents outside the city. While the adults feast on pastries and delicacies, children dressed in flamenco costumes entertain them.

During Holy Week ceremonies in Seville, parishioners wearing the long robes and pointed caps of the Inquisitors accompany processions through the city.

Local Festivals

Seville is not the only place in Spain that has a citywide *fiesta* ("festival"). At the least, every Spanish village, no matter how tiny, celebrates the feast of its special saint. Most festivals include parades, bullfights, and fireworks. Some towns hold beauty contests or light bonfires. Many have exciting special celebrations that often attract tourists from around the world. In Valencia, huge plaster figures of famous people are marched through the streets and then burned for their festival named *Fallas*. In Andalusia, for the *Romería del Rocío*, people from miles around travel by covered wagon, on horseback, and on foot to the shrine of Our Lady of "El Rocío" ("the dew"). The people wear traditional Andalusian costumes and sing as they travel. For three days they camp out, picnicking and praying all night long. In Alicante, on the Feast of the Moors and the Christians, a mock battle is held. (It's easy to guess which side wins!) Jerez de la Frontera, a city which produces fine sherry wine, has a harvest festival every September. The grapes are brought before a statue of Saint Gines, where a priest blesses them and prays that the crop will be a good one. The city also sponsors a writing contest during the harvest season. Prizes are given to essays which praise various types of sherry.

Besides town festivals, many trades and profes-

People prepare to parade these giant statues through the streets during a fiesta in Burgos.

sional groups also celebrate the feast of their patron saint. On Saint Joseph's Day, for example, carpenters might have a holiday and attend special ceremonies, since Saint Joseph was a carpenter. Students are honored on the feast of Saint Thomas Aquinas, a famous scholar. No one has classes on that day, and many families cook special meals to please their own young scholars.

The Running of the Bulls

The Fiesta of San Fermin at Pamplona is one of the most famous and exciting in Spain. From July 7 through 14, young men gather in Pamplona from all parts of Spain, and even from around the world. For one week, each man wears his swiftest shoes, his loosest clothing, and his bravest smile. That week, bands begin to play throughout the city every morning at 5:45 a.m., and there is dancing and singing in the streets. A little later, the young men gather in front of a large wooden corral on one side of the city. Inside the corral are bulls, each weighing over a thousand pounds and each extremely dangerous.

Soon a rocket goes off and the corral is opened. The men begin to run, and so do the bulls! They follow a course between wooden barriers through the streets of Pamplona. All along the way, crowds watch from windows, balconies, and sidewalks. Since the bulls are just as frightened as the men they are chasing, few stop to charge the slower runners. However, in some years men are injured or even killed during the festival of San Fermin.

After a few minutes, the runners arrive at their destination—Pamplona's bullring. The bulls are steered into a separate pen, and young cows are led into the ring. (The cows are used because they are less dangerous.) For the next hour or so, the runners get a chance to act out every Spanish child's dream. With a cape, or perhaps with just a jacket or a scarf, they tease the animals and show their own courage. They become bullfighters.

National Holidays

Many of the days on which schools and offices close are holy days of the Roman Catholic church or are the feast days of saints. Corpus Christi (Christ the King), the Assumption of Mary, All Saints' Day, and the Feast of the Immaculate Conception are celebrated throughout Spain, as are Santiago (St. James') Day and the saint's day of King Juan Carlos.

Other holidays bring to mind Spain's history. On July 18, Spaniards observe the anniversary of the Civil War. Like the war itself, this holiday often divides Spain into two groups. Those who supported Franco may march in fading uniforms, or cheer parades made up of tanks and soldiers. Republicans, or those who are too young to have participated in the fighting, may prefer to ignore the occasion. There is one thing for everyone in Spain to celebrate, however. On July 18, employers are required to give their workers half their monthly pay as a bonus. (They must make a similar payment at Christmas.)

In the United States, October 12 is celebrated as Columbus Day. This is also a holiday in Spain, but it is called Hispanic Day. The nation honors its most famous explorer as well as its ties with Spanish-speaking countries around the world. In addition, October 12 is the feast of the Virgin del Pilar, one of the patron saints of Spain. So there is double reason to celebrate.

Christmas

By December, children all over Spain are already making up lists of gifts they want from the Three Kings. Recently, some children have also begun to follow foreign customs. They write to Papa Noel (Santa Claus) too, hoping that their parents will decide to give them gifts on both Christmas and the Day of the Three Kings! However, Christmas is not traditionally a day of presents and parties, as it is in America. The focus is on the religious meaning of the day.

Shortly before Christmas, most families display a *belén*—a model of a stable, complete with animals, straw, shepherds, wise men, and of course, Jesus, Mary, and Joseph. Some families buy ready-made stables, but in others, the children construct a homemade version using plaster figures, paper straw, foil stars, and perhaps a little cotton snow. Churches also have belénes during the Christmas season and sometimes children dress in costume to make a living display in church.

On Christmas Eve, which is called "The Good Night" in Spanish, families gather around their belénes to sing Christmas carols. Later in the evening, many attend "The Rooster Mass." This religious ceremony begins at midnight, the first moment of Christmas morning. The mass gets its unusual name from the fact that roosters crow to signal the start of a new day.

Christmas Day itself is usually spent quietly, although often family and friends get together for a festive meal. Dessert is often a cake shaped like a fish, a symbol of faith. Children also eat candy made of marzipan (almond paste) and *turrón*, a hard candy traditionally served at Christmas. At this time of year, many families also serve a cake with a toy baked inside. The child who receives the piece of cake containing the toy is then named king or queen for the day.

There is one more holiday before another new year begins with twelve grapes and twelve strokes of the clock. On December 28, "The Day of the Innocents," Spanish children often play tricks on their elders. As on April Fools' Day in America, everyone must be careful on December 28. If someone borrows money, for example, he or she may remark, "May the Holy Innocents pay you . . ." Of course, the sentence is easy to finish: " . . .because I won't!"

6. *Spaniards at Home*

A popular saying in Spain is that Spaniards "eat all day and some of the night." Of course, this isn't true—no one really eats *all* day. However, Spaniards do manage to scatter a lot of snacks and meals throughout each twenty-four-hour period!

For adults the day begins, as it does in many countries, with a cup of coffee. Spanish coffee is *expresso.* Later in the day, Spaniards will have their coffee in tiny cups, because expresso is an extremely strong coffee, and a little goes a long way. Then, expresso can be taken *solo* (alone) or *cortado* (cut) with a spoonful of milk. Since in the morning these beverages are too harsh for most Spaniards, they use a large cup (almost like a bowl) and drink a half-and-half mixture of coffee and hot milk.

Many young children have hot chocolate instead of coffee for breakfast. Spanish hot chocolate is very thick, like a kind of soupy pudding. The perfect partner for chocolate is a *churro,* a long, thin, fried doughnut that scoops up the chocolate as efficiently as a spoon. However, many people have just a piece of bread with their coffee or chocolate. This is more filling than it sounds, since Spanish bread is almost a meal in itself.

Some Spanish houses are built around courtyards.

The crust is very thick and crisp, and the inside is dense and tasty. Many Spaniards enjoy it so much that they eat a piece with almost every meal.

Dinner is not until 2:00 p.m., but everyone is hungry by mid-morning, so Spaniards have a snack at about 11:00 a.m. Children eat this during their school recess; adults take a break from work. The most common snack is a *bocadillo*. Bocadillo means "little bite," but this treat is far from little. It's a roll stuffed with eggs, sausage, fried fish, or cheese.

Dinner *(comida)* is the main meal of the day. Until recently, schools, offices, and stores closed for a three-hour lunch break. With three hours, almost everyone was able to return home to eat. Now most Spaniards have only an hour-and-a-half or two hours free, so many eat in restaurants near their offices or stay in school. (Stores, except for a few department stores, still remain closed from about 1:00 to 5:00 each day.) Dinner usually begins with a bowl of soup, followed by a piece of fish. Next is a meat and vegetable course, and last is dessert—often fresh fruit or pudding.

When dinner is over, Spaniards face a long stretch until supper. Most people have another snack, or *merienda*, in the late afternoon. At home, this is likely to be a piece of cake or a pastry; Spaniards still enjoy many of the almond-and-honey sweets the Moors introduced into their country centuries ago.

In the late afternoon, city people often join friends for a *chateo*—a tour of several restaurants. No one sits down during a chateo. Instead, at each restaurant the group stands at the bar and orders very small glasses of wine called *chatos*. On the bar are plates of *tapas*, or appetizers. Tapas might be bits of egg, roasted meat, pickled vegetables, or unusual dishes like octopus cooked in ink. Everyone drinks a chato and eats a tapa. Then the group moves on to the next place. Each restaurant has a few specialties, so by moving around the diners end up with a varied menu.

The last meal of the day is supper *(cena)* which is eaten at about 10:00 p.m. Cena is usually very light—perhaps just an omelette and a salad or a plate of soup and a piece of fruit.

Famous Dishes

Most Americans confuse Spanish food with peppery Mexican cooking. Surprisingly, Spanish food is not spicy at all. Spanish cooks depend on extremely fresh ingredients instead of strong seasonings to make their dishes taste good. Few people buy more than one day's food in advance, and almost everyone shops in small stores that sell just one type of food. There are very few supermarkets in Spain; a cook preparing a meal will go to a butcher shop, a fish store, a fruit

Garlic is a popular ingredient in Spanish cooking.

stand, a dairy store, and perhaps an egg store. In these small shops it is easier to find top-quality supplies.

The most common ingredients in Spanish cooking are olive oil and garlic. In Andalusia, these are combined with tomatoes and other vegetables to make a cold soup called *gazpacho*. Gazpacho is very refreshing during the hot summers of southern Spain. Here is an easy recipe for this soup.

Gazpacho

1 medium cucumber
1 small onion
1 clove garlic (1 piece from a whole bulb)
1 green bell pepper
3 large tomatoes
2 slices of day-old bread
2 cups water
2 tablespoons wine vinegar
1/4 teaspoon salt
2 tablespoons olive oil
1 tablespoon tomato paste

1. Peel the cucumber, the onion, and the garlic clove. Cut open the bell pepper and remove the seeds and stems. Crush the garlic clove with the back of a spoon. Chop all three vegetables into one-inch pieces. Place all in a large bowl.

2. Chop the tomatoes into one-inch pieces into the bowl.

3. Crumble the bread into crumbs with your hands. Add to the vegetables.

4. Add the water, the vinegar, and the salt to the bowl and mix.

5. Using a blender or a food processor, blend all the ingredients until they are smooth. (Ask an adult for help if you've never used one of these machines before.) If there is too much for the machine, blend the soup in small batches.

6. Put the soup back in the bowl and add the olive oil and tomato paste. Blend well.

7. Refrigerate the soup at least two hours. Mix before serving.

Although it is not famous outside of Spain, the most popular dish on the peninsula is probably the *Tortilla Española*—an omelette of potatoes and eggs. This is how to make one.

Tortilla Española

1 medium-sized potato
3 eggs
1/8 teaspoon salt
olive oil

1. Peel the potato and cut it into cubes about one-half inch on a side.

2. Break the eggs into a bowl, sprinkle with salt, and beat until they are completely scrambled.

3. Cover the bottom of a small frying pan with a thin film of olive oil. Heat the oil over medium heat for a minute, before putting the potato cubes in the pan. Cook them until they get soft, stirring occasionally.

4. Pour the eggs into the pan and cook until the bottom sets. Lift the edges of the tortilla (omelette) to let the liquid egg run off the top to the bottom.

5. When the bottom is lightly browned, slide the tortilla onto a plate and cover it with another plate. Turn the plates upside down and slide the tortilla back into the pan. Cook until the other side is firm and lightly browned.

6. Remove from heat. The tortilla can be cut into wedges like a pie and served hot or cold. You can also put a piece inside a small roll to make a bocadillo.

Another famous dish from Spain is *paella*, a mixture of seafood, meat, vegetables, and rice. The rice is

Many Spaniards enjoy paella, a mixture of seafood, meat, vegetables, and rice.

seasoned with a yellow spice called saffron. It is cooked in a wide, flat pan. When the paella is brought to the table, a plate of salad is placed in the middle of the pan. Diners begin at the edge of the pan and eat their way towards the middle—right from the pot. When the salad is done the plate is removed, and everyone finishes off the middle of the paella.

Here is a popular Spanish dessert, *flan*. This is a somewhat complicated recipe; you may want to ask an adult's help.

Flan

3 whole eggs
3 egg yolks
1-1/4 cups sugar
2 cups milk
1 cup heavy whipping cream
1/2 teaspoon vanilla extract

1. Preheat the oven to 350°.

2. In a bowl, beat the eggs, the yolks, and 1/4 cup of the sugar together until thick and creamy.

3. Using a small pan, combine the milk and the whipping cream. Heat it until it is ready to bubble, but is not boiling. Beating all the time, add the hot milk to the egg-and-sugar mixture. When the two are mixed, beat in the vanilla. Set the bowl aside.

4. In a heavy saucepan, heat the remaining 1 cup

of sugar on very low heat until it begins to melt. Stir the sugar as it is melting. It will turn into a light-brown syrup, or caramel, in five to eight minutes. Be sure it doesn't burn.

5. Carefully pour the caramel into six ovenproof custard cups, one at a time. Tilt each cup so that the hot caramel coats the sides and bottoms of the cups.

6. When the caramel has set in the dishes, divide the egg-and-milk mixture evenly among the custard cups.

7. Fill a large baking pan half full of water. Set the cups in the pan. Cover the pan with aluminum foil. Bake at 350° for 45 to 50 minutes, until a knife inserted in the center of the custard comes out clean.

8. Cool the flans until you can just handle the dishes. Run a knife around the edge of each cup and turn the cup upside down onto a dessert plate or over a bowl.

9. Serve the flan at room temperature or chilled.

Here is a recipe for the hot chocolate that is a popular breakfast drink for children.

Spanish Hot Chocolate

1/2 cup unsweetened powdered cocoa
1 cup sugar
2 tablespoons plus 1 teaspoon cornstarch
1/4 cup water
1 quart milk

1. Blend the sugar and the cocoa together thoroughly.

2. In a medium-sized saucepan, dissolve the cornstarch in the water. Add the cocoa and sugar and stir until a smooth paste is made.

3. Over medium heat, stir this mixture; then add the milk little by little, stirring with a whisk as you do.

4. Simmer the chocolate, stirring it frequently, for about 10 minutes. Serve hot.

Spanish hot chocolate is so thick you may have to use a spoon to eat it!

Although Spain recently set an official drinking age limit, few Spaniards observe it at home. As they have for years, many Spaniards serve wine to their children. The red wine is mixed with lots of seltzer water, and as the child gets older, the amount of wine increases and the amount of water decreases.

Many older children and adults don't use glasses at meals; instead, they pass a *porrón* or a *bota* around. A porrón is a glass pitcher with a long spout. A bota is a leather bag with a tight-fitting top. A porrón is used in the house, while botas are good for picnics or for traveling, when an open jar might spill. When a bota or a porrón is tilted, the wine inside flows out in a stream. With practice it is possible to catch the stream in your mouth without touching the container and without spilling a single drop. However, most beginners find it is safer to put several napkins under their chins!

Grapes grow well in the warm climate, and many people drink wine with meals. In Andalusia, red wine is mixed with oranges, lemons, other fruits, and sugar to make a punch called *sangría.* Before dinner, many Spaniards also enjoy a glass of sherry, a special blended wine. Sherry is produced in the city of Jerez, which gave its name to the beverage. Some Spaniards also drink cognac, a strong wine, alone or mixed with a cup of expresso.

No Time for Sleeping

With supper at 10:00 p.m., few Spaniards feel ready to go to bed until almost midnight, and anyone who goes out after supper is awake until two or three in the morning. Even young children stay up until 11:00 or 11:30. Also, the traditional *siesta* or nap after dinner is no longer possible because the dinner break is shorter. This means that today Spaniards don't spend much time sleeping during the week, since everyone has to get up for work or school early in the morning. One Spanish writer joked about this schedule: he said the Civil War was really caused by lack of sleep! In reality, Spanish hours are not as tiring as they seem. Even without a siesta, the long lunch time and frequent breaks are relaxing. No one is as tired in the evening as they would be after an American work day.

Also, Spanish families are very close, and they share responsibilities. This prevents any one member from becoming overworked. Grandparents often live with their grown sons and daughters or at least nearby. They help out by minding the children or by doing light chores. In return, they receive help from the family when they are ill or when they need some heavy work done. There are very few nursing homes for the elderly in Spain; most older people have a useful role in the family and in the community.

Spanish families are very close. Older members often help by looking after young children.

This is easy to see in Spain's small villages. For example, in Binaced, a tiny town in Aragon, the older people often sit in the plaza during the day. The grandmothers sew or slice vegetables for dinner. Most wear black dresses, because it is the custom in Spain for women to mourn relatives who have died by giving up colored clothes. The grandfathers mend small pieces of machinery or care for the family's chickens. The mothers, who for the most part do not hold outside jobs, are busy about the house. Their husbands work in the fields or in the town's small businesses. The young children play under the watchful eyes of the older people and wait for their older brothers and sisters to return from school.

Binaced is small, and everyone knows everyone else. At dinner time, children usually eat in whatever house they are closest to. No one worries about a few extra guests! This is true throughout Spain. A Spanish host or hostess is likely to say, "My house is yours" or "You are in your own house" to every visitor—and then act as if it were true. Nothing is too good for a guest; the best food, bed, and entertainment are given freely, even if the family itself has to do without.

The Church and Everyday Life

Almost everyone in Spain is Catholic, and the church plays an important role in everyday life. All the major events in life—birth, marriage, and death—are marked by religious ceremonies. In fact, until recently the only marriage ceremony permitted in Spain was a Catholic one, and divorce was illegal.

In most villages, the church is an important social center as well. Children go there for religious instruc-

The Catholic church is very important in Spanish life. Rural churches are often social centers as well.

tion, choir practice, and youth groups. Adults meet after services to exchange greetings with their neighbors; many also belong to church-sponsored clubs. The entire town attends Sunday services. The children sit together in a special section.

Spaniards are generally named after saints. However, the saint's name is only the beginning. Spanish names follow a complicated pattern.

Let's take an imaginary child named Maria. Her mother's name was Sanchez and her father's name was Díaz. Maria will have two last names, one from her father and one from her mother. The father's is written first, and if anyone is in a hurry the mother's is not used. So this child is called Maria Díaz Sanchez, or Maria Díaz for short.

Suppose Maria marries José Galdos Rodriguez when she grows up. He keeps his name, and she does, too. However, she may also be called *la señora de Galdos*—the wife of Galdos. For formal occasions, she can use the whole name: Maria Díaz Sanchez de Galdos. (And that's not even counting middle names!) Maria's and José's children will use the last names of both parents: Galdos Díaz.

Maria and José may also receive a special title from young children or anyone who wants to show them respect. *Don* and *Doña* are similar to "Sir" and "Ma'am" in English. They are only used with first names, so our imaginary couple would be Doña Maria and Don José.

Although this system of names is very complicated, Spaniards are used to it. Everyone knows who he or she is! Because the Spanish home, church, and family life are still rooted in tradition, everyone also knows his or her place in society.

7. *School Days*

Every school day, thousands of Spanish students file into the classrooms of the University of Salamanca. For the most part, these young people could not be more up-to-date. There are lots of blue jeans and radios blaring rock music, and an occasional punk ponytail or streak of orange hair. In other words, it's a university scene that could be almost anywhere in the world.

There is one difference, however. The university these students are attending is over 750 years old. Today's punk rockers walk along the same halls where young Spaniards discussed philosophy in the Middle Ages. They sit at desks carved with the initials of scholars who studied there during the sixteenth century. They visit classrooms where professors once lectured with members of the Inquisition watching from the back of the room.

Old Schools, New Schools

Students at the University of Salamanca may wander through historic halls, but most Spanish students have exactly the opposite experience—their schools are likely to be extremely new. That's because Spain is opening more and more schools every year. Some are in buildings that were once convents, factories, or even castles. Others are in modern buildings whose paint is hardly dry when the first children arrive to meet their new teachers.

There are two types of schools in Spain, state-run and private. Most private schools are sponsored by the Catholic church, and are usually either all-male or all-female. State schools generally accept both boys and girls. Tuition is paid by the government in all schools, although children in private schools must pay extra fees. This can be quite expensive. Extra fees are charged at one private school for medical exams, sports, teaching materials, information bulletins, insurance, PTA dues, a swimming pool, testing materials, and maintenance of equipment.

No matter which type of school they attend, all children must buy their own books. Texts are not lent out and returned at the end of the term as they are in some United States schools. Grants are sometimes given to students from poor families who cannot afford the book bills.

Most young children wear uniforms to school. Boys usually wear a one-piece overall which is blue, brown, or white. Some boys wear pants with a belted smock on top. Girls dress in apronlike pinafores made of plain or striped light-colored cloth. Sometimes the children wear embroidered name badges on the front of the uniforms. This makes it easier to learn who's who! Like children everywhere, Spanish kids like to play, and their uniforms show it. September's neat, spotless outfits are usually fairly ragged by June.

First and Second Stage Schools

Currently, Spanish law requires children to attend school from ages six to fourteen. However, a few parents send their sons and daughters to nursery school at the age of three, and even more enroll their children at four or five. As in American nursery schools, the children paint, work with clay, and learn some numbers and letters. Now that "El Barrio Sesamo" ("Sesame Street") is on Spanish TV, many children come to school already able to count and name the letters of the alphabet.

At the age of six, students begin the *Primera Etapa* (First Stage) of their official schooling. This lasts until age eleven. During these years, the children stay in one room with the same teacher all day. From ages twelve to fourteen, the children are in the *Segunda Etapa* (Second Stage). Though they remain in the same building, they now change teachers for each subject.

Spanish children spend a lot more time in school than do American children. In a typical Spanish school

Young children often attend nursery school where they paint, draw, and learn numbers and letters.

of the first or second stages, students arrive around 8:30 a.m. They play in an enclosed patio (like a schoolyard) until the bell rings at 9:00. Then the children form lines and follow their teachers into the building. They have classes until about 11:00, and then a half-hour outdoor recess. Many children eat a small snack before returning for another hour of classes. Then it's time for lunch. Since the next lesson does not begin until 3:00 p.m., there is enough time for most students to go home for lunch. Those who stay in the building are served a hot

In the Segunda Etapa, children study many subjects. These students are working on a math problem with their teacher.

meal in the school's dining room. A typical menu might include rice, fish, salad, and cookies; or beans, potatoes, meatballs, and fruit. Then the children are given games to amuse themselves with until their classmates return from home. A popular pastime is table soccer, which has a board as a field and little players mounted on long, metal rods. One child stands at each end of the board and moves the players up and down the field.

In the afternoon, the students study for two more hours, with a half-hour break. At 5:30, most children head home for the day; those who have fallen behind in their work stay for an extra hour of instruction. As if this schedule were not long enough, Spanish children also have a half-day of school on Saturdays!

Most of the subjects Spanish children study are similar to those in American schools. Naturally, Spanish replaces English. Schools in Catalonia, Galicia, and the Basque province also teach their province's language. Second-stage children take a foreign language (usually English or French) and may have a course called "Pre-technology." In pre-technology, the students learn to make models, to construct simple machines, and to do craftwork. All pupils study religion in both state and private schools. At one time, only Catholicism was taught, but now the children learn about many different faiths. Students also take gym, which includes sports like volleyball, basketball, and soccer, as well as first aid instruction, hiking, and map-reading. Unfortunately, most Spanish schools are built without playing fields, so the children must play sports in their school's patio.

The following chart shows one fourteen-year-old's schedule for the last year of the second stage.

	9:00-10:00	10:00-11:00	11:00-11:30	11:30-12:30	3:00-4:00	4:00-4:30	4:30-5:30
MONDAY	Spanish	Math	Recess	Foreign Language (English)	Science	Recess	Art
TUESDAY	Math	Spanish	Recess	Social Studies	Gym	Recess	Gym
WEDNESDAY	Spanish	Math	Recess	Foreign Language (English)	Religion	Recess	Social Studies
THURSDAY	Math	Spanish	Recess	Religion	Science	Recess	Art
FRIDAY	Spanish	Math	Recess	Foreign Language (English)	Gym	Recess	Social Studies
SATURDAY	Music, Drama, or Pre-technology				No School		
SUNDAY	No School All Day						

Bachillerato

At the age of fourteen, students who do not intend to go on to college may attend a technical school There, they learn skills such as auto mechanics and prepare for a non-college career. Pre-college students enter *bachillerato*, which is a type of high school. At this stage, there are no uniforms, and everyone must pay tuition in both state and private schools.

During the four years of bachillerato, a student may take courses in Spanish, math, foreign languages, history, science, religion, gym, social studies, crafts, and home economics. Bachillerato is organized like an American high school, but there are some differences. Students address their teachers in a formal way, calling them Don ____________ or Doña ____________ or using the title "*Profesor.*" The pupils stand when they answer a question, and they may be required to sit with their arms folded when they are not writing.

Grading Systems

The illustration on page 122 shows a report card for a ten-year-old Spanish child in the first stage. As you see, teachers do not use the letter grade system. A child may receive the following marks: *Muy Deficiente* (very unsatisfactory), *Insuficiente* (unsatisfactory), *Suficiente* (satisfactory), *Bien* (good), *Notable* (very good), and *Sobresaliente* (outstanding). On this report card, Vanesa Moles was rated outstanding in Spanish, math, science, and social studies; very good in religion and art; and good in physical education.

The same system of marks continues into bachillerato. In some schools, students receive progress reports every week, with formal marks given after final exams at the end of the year. The same final exam is given in every school of the province. This is to make sure that all Spanish schools follow the required course of instruction. Although no one likes

BOLETIN DE EVALUACION FINAL	ALUMNO	No. AL	CLASE	CURSO	SECC.
	MOLES DEFIOR, VANESA	39	39	5	A

CENTRO	CORRESPONDENCIA	ENSEÑANZA
COLEGIO PUBLICO "SIERRA NEVADA" GRANADA 6908		C. ME No. MATRICULA FECHA 21-6-83

MATERIAS	CALIFICACION FINAL	EVALUACIONES 1	2	3	4	5	6	PENDIENTES DE RECUPERAR
LENGUA CASTELLANA	SOBRESALIENTE							
MATEMATICAS	SOBRESALIENTE							
CIENCIAS NATURALEZA	SOBRESALIENTE							
CIENCIAS SOCIALES	SOBRESALIENTE							
ENS. RELIGIOSA-ETICA	NOTABLE							
EDUCACION ARTISTICA	NOTABLE							
EDUCACION FISICA	BIEN							

CALIFICACION GLOBAL DEL CURSO: SOBRESALIENTE

OBSERVACIONES DE LA JUNTA DE EVALUACION

*LAS MATERIAS SEÑALADAS CON ASTERISCO INDICAN PENDIENTES DE RECUPERAR   LAS MATERIAS SEÑALADAS CON SIGNO + HAN SIDO RECUPERADAS

finals, Spanish students have no reason to be afraid at the end of the year. Children who fail their final exams are not left back. Instead, they are given extra work over the summer and during the regular school year so they can catch up with their classmates.

Going to the University

After bachillerato, students who plan to go on to college enroll in a one-year preparation course. They take the same subjects the bachillerato offers but on a higher level. They may also take a course which introduces various career fields like law, medicine, or education. At the end of the year, there is a final. Students who fail may take one or two more years of college preparation until they are ready for the university.

How would you like to go to a school with a hundred thousand other young people? That's how many students attend the University of Madrid. Another fifty thousand are registered at the Central University of Barcelona. However, not all Spanish universities are that large. Some "small" Spanish colleges have only five thousand students.

With numbers like these, it is clear that Spanish professors cannot get to know every one of their students. They may have classes with as many as one thousand young men and women registered! University teachers rely on lectures and readings to present their ideas, and final exams to check on their students' success.

Some students live at home and travel daily to class, but others live in dormitories or *colegios*—residences for students. The colegio provides the personal contact that the university classes cannot supply. Students who live there share homework and studies with each other and with their houseparents, who try to make the colegio a kind of "home away from home" for their charges. Colegios sponsor concerts, parties, lectures,

College students like these young women will receive a Licenciado degree after five years of advanced study.

and clubs for their students. Most colegios have a café or bar where students can unwind after classes.

For those students who live out in the country and cannot attend classes at all, the education department has recently begun long-distance colleges. These students receive lessons in the mail or by way of radio or television.

The university course lasts five years, when a *Licenciado* degree is awarded. Students can also receive a lesser degree after three years. Those who wish to continue after their Licenciado is complete can study for a *Doctorado* (Doctorate) degree, which takes two years.

In the past, students who wished to study advanced or very technical subjects often had to go to other countries because the schools in Spain were not good. The Spanish government was aware of this problem. In fact, better education has been the goal of all the Spanish governments since before the Civil War. At the beginning of this century, only the children of wealthy Spaniards were well educated. Most peasants could not read and write at all. The Republic opened thousands of new schools, but even this was not enough to provide places for all Spanish children. Also, many children who did have a school nearby were unable to attend, even though their presence was required by law. Their families were so poor that the labor of everyone was needed just to survive.

The Franco government continued the effort to improve education. By 1952, 72 percent of Spain's school-age children were being educated. Twenty years later, the number had jumped to 96 percent. Now, nearly all eligible children are in school. Moreover, the schools themselves have been improved. Future Spanish engineers, architects, doctors, and other professionals can now find all the training they need right in their own country.

8. *Bullfights and* Star Wars

The sun blazes on a golden circle of sand. In the center of the circle, a man dressed in tight-fitting pants and a jewelled jacket stands holding a cape. Fifty yards away is a huge bull. Quietly, the man twirls the cape. The creature, and everyone in the crowd, watches carefully. Suddenly the bull charges! The crowd rises to its feet as the *matador* faces death in the form of a thousand pounds of muscle, two sharp horns, and lightning hooves. Cheers explode: the matador steps aside at the very last second, and the bull runs harmlessly past.

The roots of bullfighting go deep into Iberian history. Even the cave artists of Altamira painted bulls, and until recently, the bullfight was every Spaniard's favorite pastime. Little boys took turns playing bull and matador with a kitchen towel. Successful bullfighters were national heroes, and newspapers reviewed each matador's performance. Long lines formed to buy the cheap *sol* (sunny) and the expensive *sombra* (shady) seats for every fight. Today, the popularity of bullfighting is lessening somewhat. Many bullfights are now attended more by tourists than by Spaniards.

One thing never changes, however. The bullfight is still surrounded by a great deal of ceremony. Each fight

Although not as popular as they once were, bullfights still attract many spectators. Here, a bull charges the matador.

begins with the matadores and their teams parading around the ring. A trumpet sounds and the bullfighters bow to the president of the arena. From his high seat, he throws down the key which unlocks the bulls' pen. The ring clears and the bull enters.

Picadores on horseback and *bandarilleros* on foot chase and wound the bull. Finally, the matador strides into the ring, and the real drama begins. The weakened bull charges again and again as the bullfighter encourages the animal to come closer and closer. Sometimes the bull manages to hurt the bullfighter with its horns. Usually, though, the man wins. At the end of the fight, the matador drives his sword through the bull's neck and into his heart, and the match is over.

Arena officials judge the matador's performance. If he has fought well, he may be awarded an ear, a hoof, or the tail of the dead bull. The crowd also shows its approval by throwing presents into the ring. After a good fight, flowers, hats, sausages, and even sweaters come showering down from the stands.

Some people are horrified by bullfights. They hate the fact that an animal is wounded and killed in the sport, and they believe that people who like watching this must be very cruel to enjoy such a show. Yet bullfight fans view their sport differently. To them, the struggle between man and an enormously powerful animal is beautiful. Although the bull nearly always loses, the animal's bravery and willingness to fight earn it the respect of the crowd. In the same way, the matador's courage and grace are important—not simply the fact that he kills the bull.

Soccer and Other Sports

Bullfights are not as popular as they used to be because many Spaniards have transferred their atten-

Soccer is popular with Spaniards of all ages.

Jai alai is a fast-paced game requiring great skill.

tion to soccer. Soccer, which is called *futbol* (football) in Spanish, plays to sellout crowds in every city. Even the tiniest village has a soccer team and on weekends, neighboring towns play each other. It is not unusual for the entire village to watch a game, probably while enjoying a picnic lunch. The proud family of a star player may even use the team photo as a Christmas card! At World Cup time, everyone clusters around television sets to cheer Spain's national team.

Another popular Spanish sport is *jai alai*, or *pelota*, which is played with a hard ball and a small, shallow basket called a *cesta*. Jai alai originated in the Basque province. It is said to be the fastest and most exhausting game in the world. Players catch the ball in their cestas and fling it against a wall. The other team must catch the lightning-fast rebound. Professionals play jai alai in a court while children often use the side of their school or church as a backstop.

Swimming, volleyball, and basketball also have many fans in Spain. Running is becoming more popular. An annual marathon is held in Madrid, and in a recent year, four thousand runners took part.

Boys and girls very seldom play together in Spain. The traditional male and female roles are still strong, and girls are often kept at home learning to cook and sew while their brothers play outside. However, girls are not completely left out of sports. They participate in volleyball, basketball, and track, but bullfighting, soccer, and jai alai remain all-male. Young girls also play a kind of jump rope with an elastic cord, and a hopscotch game with soda caps. Both boys and girls ride bikes on the street or in their schoolyards.

The youngest children, both boys and girls, enjoy games like cops and robbers. The "cops" chase the

Spaniards and tourists from all over the world enjoy water sports at the many beautiful beaches of Spain.

"robbers," and after the arrest is made, the roles are reversed. Spanish kids also play tag, hide-and-seek, and board games like Monopoly and Parcheesi. Just recently, video games became the newest rage!

On the City Streets

Another Spanish passion is gambling. Spaniards will bet on anything, but the biggest gamble of all, the lottery, is tied to sports. Each week, Spaniards may buy lottery tickets that predict the outcome of fourteen soccer games—win, lose, or tie. Prizes are enormous if only one person has chosen the correct combination of winning teams. If several people are right, the money is shared. Books and magazine articles frequently advise Spaniards how to choose the winning and losing teams, and most lottery players are willing to explain their personal system. However, one of the biggest prizes ever given was won by a woman who knew nothing at all about soccer. She had simply asked the butcher to chop her meat fourteen times. Each time he raised the cleaver she said, "Win, lose, or tie," and wrote down the word she was saying when the cleaver hit the meat!

Another soccer lottery is held each week to benefit the Spanish Organization for the Blind. Blind men and women pin tickets they are selling to their jackets. They call, "For today, for today, buy two for today!" as they walk through the streets. This unusual lottery is not a charity. It is a business run by the blind for the blind. Blind people not only sell the tickets, but also organize the drawings, award the prizes, and spend the profits on salaries and projects for each other.

Lottery ticket sellers are not the only vendors in the streets. Spaniards pushing carts offer ice cream, nuts, pastries, and tobacco. During very hot weather in the South of Spain, it is even possible to find a water seller! All these vendors are in the streets because at certain times of day, that is the easiest place to find a crowd of Spaniards. Spaniards of all ages love a *paseo*—a long, slow walk through the center of town. There they meet neighbors and friends, exchange the latest gossip, and show off new clothes. Married couples stroll arm in arm, teenagers flirt with each other, and young children race up and down ahead of their parents.

Late afternoon is the most common time for a paseo, and many people also go out on Sunday mornings after mass. In Madrid, Sunday walkers may wander through the *rastro*, an open-air flea market. The rastro is famous for selling anything and everything: a pile of fashion magazines from 1898 may sit on top of new sponges and kitchen towels. Bargain hunters have a wonderful time at the rastro.

Shoppers can find anything and everything at the rastro in Madrid.

C. CAMINO
MUEBLES
C. CAMINO
PROMEX
TUS NUEVOS

Cafés, Tertulias, and Discos

No one can walk all the time, and one of the best parts of a paseo is a stop in a café. Spaniards love to watch what's going on, so in all but the coldest weather, cafés put tables outdoors. There, customers may sit for hours, watching the paseo and sipping a cup of coffee or a glass of wine. No waiter will annoy them by asking them to order more since in Spain it is expected that life goes on at a leisurely pace.

In the corner of some cafés, people gather in the evening for a *tertulia.* A tertulia is an informal "talking club." The members never ask to join and never plan when they are going to meet next. They seem to drift together every so often. Yet tertulias can become permanent institutions. One tertulia in Madrid met once a week for over thirty years! The topics discussed in a tertulia depend on the members. Farmers are likely to argue about the price of olive oil or the best method for fertilizing orange trees. Business executives and students may tackle politics, religion, or the weather. Some tertulias change subjects each week; others are organized according to interest. Visitors to the café may sometimes choose between several types of tertulias.

In the Basque country, many "talking clubs" are also "eating clubs." Basque men (never women) go to clubhouses in the evening to cook a big, fancy

Cafés are excellent spots for meeting friends or watching the paseo.

meal. Every member takes turns doing the dishwashing chores, and the cook is a different man each night. No matter how much the group enjoys a particular meal, every member is sure that his recipe is clearly better than the one the cook used!

Younger Spaniards are more likely to be found in a discotheque than in a tertulia or eating club. It has been said that Spain has more discos than any other European country. The crowds begin to gather a few hours after supper (around midnight) and they dance until three or four in the morning. American and British rock-and-roll music are the favorites, although Spanish pop tunes are also played.

Television, Theater, and Movies

Spaniards who are not out on a paseo or arguing in a tertulia are likely to be home watching television. Spain has two channels that broadcast in Castilian. There are also channels for speakers of Catalan, Galician, and Euskera. All channels are run by TVE, the Spanish government's television agency.

What do Spaniards watch? Just about all the same kinds of programs Americans do: there are news and information shows, sporting events (mostly soccer, but also important bullfights), and entertainment. Spanish TV also broadcasts many concerts of Spanish music, as well as a Catholic mass every Sunday. As in the United States, the most popular shows are often movies that appeared in theaters a few years earlier. Many of the movies and shows are imported from other countries, but the sound track is translated into Spanish. TV listings may include such programs as "Sesame Street," "Dynasty," and "The Pink Panther."

Going out to the movies is also a favorite Spanish pastime. In cities, the theaters resemble those of the United States. In small villages, the meeting room of the town hall or an open-air tent may become a theater on weekends. Spanish children enjoy all the same movies that American kids go to; Walt Disney movies and *Star Wars* are special favorites.

All large cities and many small ones also have live theater performances. Actors present the great classics of Spanish theater as well as modern plays from Spain and other countries. Ticket prices for plays are fairly low; students who have very little spending money often ask for a seat "in heaven." That's the last row or two next to the ceiling of the theater, close to the sky!

The popularity of the theater is just one example of a fact that is also shown in Spanish devotion to sports, tertulias, paseos, and other pastimes: Spaniards know how to enjoy life!

9. *Adventure in America*

One of the first Spanish immigrants to the New World started a very long walk one day. Álvar Núñez Cabeza de Vaca was shipwrecked in the Gulf of Mexico in 1528. When he came ashore on Galveston Island near the coast of Texas, he was captured by the Karakawa Indians. The Indians made Cabeza de Vaca their slave, but he soon gained a reputation among them as a medicine man. After seven years with the Karakawas, Cabeza de Vaca escaped and began to walk west. Many months later, he reached a Spanish mission in Mexico. Álvar Núñez Cabeza de Vaca had traveled across half of the United States on foot!

This journey was only one of the adventures that America had in store for Spaniards. When Cabeza de Vaca returned to Spain, he told everyone about "the seven cities of Cibola," which were said to be made of gold. Hernando De Soto heard these tales and decided to search for the treasure. De Soto traveled throughout the southeastern United States, taking many valuables along the way. One Indian chief gave him over three hundred pounds of pearls! However, Hernando De Soto never found the golden cities. (And for good reason: they did not exist!)

Francisco de Coronado also set out to find Cibola, searching in what is now Arizona, New Mexico, Texas, and Kansas. His expedition began in 1540 and included three hundred soldiers, seven hundred Indian slaves, a thousand horses, and many other animals and supplies. Coronado did find a "Cibola," but not the one he had been dreaming about for so long. Instead of golden cities, he discovered seven small Zuni Indian villages and the Indians' most valuable possessions were straw huts and corn.

Although these Spaniards' journeys through America did not turn out the way they expected, their expeditions were not failures. Cabeza de Vaca, De Soto, and Coronado were the first Europeans to explore the southern United States. They claimed all the land they traveled through for Spain. This added vast colonies to the Spanish Empire—colonies whose natural resources were even more valuable than the legendary treasures of Cibola could ever have been.

Of course, the land claimed by these explorers, as well as most of the treasure and resources sent back to Spain, belonged to native American Indian peoples. Many times the Spaniards fought bloody battles with the Indians to obtain them. Whole cultures such as the Aztec civilization of Mexico and the Incas of Peru were destroyed by Spanish troops, who were sometimes helped by Indian rivals of those cultures. Native people were killed or enslaved, in many cases, and cities were leveled so that new settlements could be built in their places.

Spanish Settlements

As Hernando De Soto and Francisco de Coronado traveled throughout the South, members of their expeditions stayed behind from time to time, creating many small settlements. De Soto himself founded Tampa Bay, Florida.

In the West, other Spanish immigrants were also colonizing California. Juan Rodríguez Cabrillo had explored and claimed the coast of California and Oregon for Spain in 1542. However, no settlements were established in that territory for two hundred years. Then a party of Spaniards traveled north from Mexico. A member of that group was Junípero Serra, a truly remarkable man.

Junípero Serra had been born on the island of Majorca in 1713. When he was sixteen, he entered a Catholic religious order and became a friar (brother). Twenty years later, he sailed for the New World to bring the message of his faith to the Indians. At first, he worked in Mexico, but in 1769 he was sent to establish Catholic missions in California. Serra had a bad leg and could only move with difficulty. In spite of

Father Junípero Serra founded many missions in California, including Mission San Carlos Borromeo at Carmel.

that fact, he spent the next fifteen years walking throughout the Southwest and West.

He first walked from Mexico to San Diego. There he built a church and started a small settlement. Then he walked north, founding a string of missions along the California coast. Each mission was one day's walk apart. Other friars joined Serra and eventually, there were twenty-one missions along a road that was named *El Camino Real*—the royal highway. Serra eventually became the head of his church in California. One of his duties was to travel from mission to mission on foot visiting his priests and converts. Although no one has added it up, Serra may have put as many miles in as Cabeza de Vaca!

If you look at a modern map of the United States, you will see the names of settlements founded by Friar Serra and other Spanish immigrants. Many are named after saints—San Francisco, Saint Augustine, San Antonio, San Jose, Santa Fe, and hundreds more. Los Angeles, Monterey, Tucson, and Albuquerque are other Spanish settlements that grew into important American cities.

A Huge Minority

Spain kept control of much of the southern United States for about three hundred years. Then in the nineteenth century, all of Spain's former lands in North America became part of the United States by treaty or sale. After the Spanish-American War in 1898, the United States took possession of Puerto Rico, Cuba, and the Philippines. Cuba and the Philippines eventually received their independence, but Puerto Rico became a commonwealth of the United States.

Many Puerto Ricans and other Hispanic people from South and Central America are descendants of the Spanish explorers and settlers of long ago. Their ancestors also include the native tribes and black slaves who were brought by the Spaniards to work in the colonies. Throughout the years, many Hispanic people have emigrated to the United States. Their many accomplishments may be included in the list of contributions Spain has made to this country.

Immigration from Spain itself did not end in the colonial days. Throughout the nineteenth century, a few thousand Spaniards arrived in the United States each year. At the beginning of the twentieth century, the pressures which eventually led to the Spanish Civil War increased. Because of this, the number of immigrants from Spain jumped dramatically. Between 1870 and 1900 (a thirty-year period), about 18,000 Spaniards moved to America. During the next thirty years, over 125,000 emigrated!

Quite a few of these new Americans came from the Basque country. Many Basques settled in the Great Basin, an area that includes parts of Utah, California, Oregon, Idaho, and Nevada. The immigrants often became shepherds or worked in other areas of the sheep industry. Today, there are ten to fifteen thousand people of Basque descent in the Great Basin. They have a "Sheepherders Ball" and a St. Ignatius Day picnic in Boise, Idaho, every year. (St. Ignatius of Loyola was born in the Basque country.)

Other Spanish immigrants have scattered throughout the United States. Often, these new Americans settle

These boys and girls perform music at a Basque club meeting in the United States.

in the Hispanic neighborhoods of major cities. Although Spanish-speaking Americans come from many countries and have different cultures and customs, their common language binds them together. In some areas, homesick Spaniards have gathered into clubs where they can enjoy some memories of their former country. In New York City, for example, *Casa Galicia* (Galicia House) is a meeting place for Galician New Yorkers. New York, like many large cities, also has Spanish television and radio stations, daily Spanish newspapers, and Spanish magazines. Their broadcasts and writings are aimed mostly at Hispanic-Americans, but they also include news of interest to Spaniards.

Unfortunately, besides sharing television shows and newspapers, Hispanic-Americans also share something else with Spanish-Americans—prejudice. In the minds of some Americans, all Spanish-speaking people are the same, and none are to be trusted. Prejudice has often been directed at immigrants. Throughout the history of the United States, each new group has faced some distrust and disapproval, especially if the group's numbers are large. Some Americans fear that the newcomers will take their jobs; others are simply baffled by the immigrants' foreign ways.

Palm Trees, Horses, and Oranges

In spite of this prejudice, America would be a much poorer country today without the contributions of Spain and Spanish-Americans. In California, for example, there once were no palm trees at all. One palm tree in San Diego tells the story. A small sign on it says, "First palm planted in California—1769, by Father Serra." Junípero Serra, like many other immigrants from Spain, brought plants and animals with him as he traveled through the New World. Oranges, lemons, limes, peaches, pears, apples, and apricots are just some of the fruit-bearing plants that are not native to the United States. All were first planted in America by Spanish immigrants. Spaniards also introduced many types of domestic animals, such as horses, cattle, sheep, and goats to the United States. (Some Indians believed that the first Spanish explorers they saw were half-human and half-animal. They had never seen a horse and rider before!)

The early Spanish colonists also brought new types of farming tools to America, and they taught other Americans their methods of caring for sheep and cattle. This had an effect on our language, too. Many of the English words cowboys use today originally came from Spanish, including lariat, lasso, bronco, corral, rodeo, chaps, cinch, ranch, and stampede. The hardworking Spaniards also brought another word to English when they rested from their labors—siesta!

Spain has also influenced American cooking. Many people have sampled sangría, paella, and Spanish omelettes. Found mostly in Louisiana, Creole cooking is a mixture of Spanish and French styles, passed down by the colonists who settled there long ago. A quick drive through southern California or the Southwest reveals another Spanish contribution. The adobe bricks, inner patios, and iron balconies of many houses are just like those in the South of Spain.

Some Famous Spanish-Americans

In the United States Capitol building in Washington, D.C., each state is allowed to erect statues of its two most honored citizens. One of the statues representing California is of Junípero Serra. Serra is not the only Spanish immigrant from that time to achieve fame in America. Pedro Menéndez de Avilés, a member of a noble Asturian family, ran away from home at the age of fourteen. He became a sailor and fought in a war between France and Spain. In 1565 the king of Spain sent Menéndez de Avilés to Florida. There he founded Saint Augustine, which is the oldest city in the United States. Other Spaniards founded and named many other cities in the South and the Southwest.

In more recent times, José Greco became the most famous flamenco dancer in the United States. Greco, whose mother was Spanish, was born in Italy in 1918. When he was very young, his family moved to America. Greco became a professional dancer and a real flamenco artist. One critic once commented that Greco danced " . . . as if he were awfully angry at the floor!" Xavier Cugat, who was born in Barcelona, Spain, in 1900, moved to Cuba when he was a boy. He eventually formed a dance band and brought Americans their first taste of Latin dancing. Pablo Casals, another native Catalonian, fled Spain during the Spanish Civil War

José Greco, here with his partner Nana Lorca, popularized flamenco dancing throughout the world.

Born in Madrid, singer Julio Iglesias today lives in Miami, Florida. His concerts are sold out wherever he performs.

and eventually settled in Puerto Rico. Casals was one of the best cellists in the world until his death in 1973. The writer Juan Ramón Jiménez also left Spain for Puerto Rico when the Republicans lost the Civil War. Jiménez's most famous work is *Platero and I*, a wonderful story about a little donkey and his master. Jiménez won the Nobel Prize for Literature in 1956. Luis Buñuel, a filmmaker, was also a war refugee. He settled in the United States in 1938 and later moved to Mexico. Another Spanish-American, Severo Ochoa, was born in Luarca, Spain, but later moved to the United States. He won the Nobel Prize for Medicine in 1959 for his work with nucleic acids. Julio Iglesias, a singer popular all over the world, but originally from Spain, today lives Miami, Florida.

Of course, there are many, many people of Spanish descent who work in every line of business in America. The United States has benefitted greatly from their hard work and their unsung contributions to American life.

There is an old Spanish proverb, "Who says 'Spain' says everything." There is a tremendous amount of variety packed into Spain's small area of land. Its people, too, reflect this variety and have brought a rich culture and a proud heritage with them when they adopted the United States as their home.

Appendix A

Castilian Spanish: A Guide to Pronunciation

The type of Spanish spoken in Spain, Castilian, differs somewhat in pronunciation from the Spanish spoken in North, South, and Central America. Spanish is rather regular in pronunciation, and almost every letter in each word is pronounced. Below is a chart showing the sounds that letters generally have in Spanish.

a	as in *papa*
b	hard *(bike)* at the beginning of a word; soft *(table)* within a word (shown as [b])
c	as in *cat*; but before *e* and *i*, sounds like the *th* in *think* (shown as [th])
ch	as in *chow*
d	as in *dawn* when at the beginning or end of a word; but sounds like the *th* in *that* when within a word
e	as in *they*
f	as in *fat*
g	as in *gas* when it begins a word or comes before the letters *a, o, u,* or after *n*; as a breathy *h* sound when it appears before the letters *e* or *i* or in the middle of a word
h	is silent
i	as in *police*
j	as a breathy *h* sound
k	as in *kernel*; only found in adopted non-Spanish words
l	as in *late*
ll	as a *y* sound

m	as in *more*
n	as in *not*; when it appears before the letters *b, v, p,* or *f*, it has an *m* sound
ñ	has a *nyuh* sound
o	as in *flow*
p	as in *open*
q	always used with *u*; *qu* as in *quite*
r	pronounced as the *tt* in *pretty* when within a word; rolled *(rrrr)* when it begins a word, appears as a double *r*, or comes before the letters *l, n,* or *s*
s	as in *sun*; but sounds like the *s* in *pose* when it comes before the letters *b, v, d, m, n, l, g,* or *r*
t	as in *stupid*
u	as in *ruler*
v	pronounced as a *b (baby)* at the beginning of a word; but as a soft *b (table)* inside a word (shown as [b])
w	not used in Spanish
x	as in *ax*; but sometimes has a *gss* sound before a consonant
y	as in *year*
z	as the *th* in *think (*shown as [th])

Special letter combinations:

ai	as the *i* in *life*	oi	as the *oy* in *toy*
au	as the *ow* in *towel*	ua	as the *wa* in *watch*
ei	as the *ay* in *way*	ui	as the *we* in *week*
ia	as *eeyah*	ue	as the *we* in *wet*
io	as *eeyoh*	uo	as the *wo* in *woke*
iu	as *eeyuh*		

Accented syllables

The accent is on the next-to-the-last syllable if the word ends in a vowel, an *n*, or an *s*.

The accent is on the last syllable when a word ends in a consonant other than an *n* or an *s*.

Accent marks are used with words if the accent varies from these two rules.

Appendix B

Spanish Embassies and Consulates in the United States and Canada

The embassies and consulates of Spain would be glad to help you learn more about Spain. They can recommend books and articles and direct you to information about traveling in their country.

U. S. Embassy and Consulates

Boston, Massachusetts
Consulate General of Spain
545 Boylston St., Suite 803
Boston, MA 02116
Phone (617) 536-2506

Chicago, Illinois
Consulate General of Spain
180 N. Michigan Ave., Suite 1905
Chicago, IL 60601
Phone (312) 782-4588

Houston, Texas
Consulate General of Spain
2411 Fountainview, Suite 130
Houston, TX 77057
Phone (713) 783-6200

Los Angeles, California
Consulate General of Spain
6300 Wilshire Blvd., Suite 1431
Los Angeles, CA 90048
Phone (213) 658-6050

Miami, Florida
Consulate General of Spain
151 Seville Ave., Second Floor
Coral Gables, FL 33134
Phone (305) 446-5511

New Orleans, Louisiana
Consulate General of Spain
2102 World Trade Center
2 Canal St.
New Orleans, LA 70130
Phone (504) 525-4951

New York, New York
Consulate General of Spain
150 E. 58th St.
New York, NY 10022
Phone (212) 355-4080

San Francisco, California
Consulate General of Spain
2080 Jefferson St.
San Francisco, CA 94123
Phone (415) 922-2995

Washington, D.C.
Embassy of Spain
2700 15th St., NW
Washington, D.C. 20009
Phone (202) 265-4939

Canadian Embassy and Consulate

Montreal, Quebec

Consulate General of Spain
1 Westmount Sq., Suite 1456
Montreal, Quebec H3Z 2P9
Phone (514) 935-2828

Ottawa, Ontario

Embassy of Spain
350 E. Sparks St., Suite 802
Ottawa, Ontario K1R 7S8
Phone (613) 237-2193

Glossary

Armada (ahr·MAH·dah)—fleet of Spanish ships defeated by the British Navy in 1588

bachillerato (bahk·ee·yuh·RAH·toh)—college preparatory high school

bandarillero (bahnd·ahr·ree·YEHR·oh)—bullfighters who challenge a bull on foot and weaken it by pushing sharp sticks into its neck

Barrio Sesamo (BAH·ree·oh say·SAH·moh), **El**—Spanish version of the TV program "Sesame Street"

belén (bay·LEHN)—Christmas decoration of a stable with figures of people and animals in it

bien (BYEHN)—good; a grade like a *C* in American schools

bocadillo (boh·kah·DEE·oh)—small stuffed snack roll

bota (BOH·tuh)—leather wine sack

Carlanco (kahr·LAHN·koh)—monster in Spanish fairy tales

cena ([TH] AY·nah)—supper, served around 10:00 p.m.

cesta ([TH] AY·stah)—shallow catching basket used in the game of jai alai

chateo (chah·TAY·oh)—Spanish custom of dropping in on a number of restaurants to eat appetizers and drink wine

chato (CHAH·toh)—small glass of wine
churro (CHOORR·oh)—thin, deep-fried doughnut
Cibola ([th] ee·BOHL·uh)—legendary place where there were seven wealthy cities
cognac (KOHN·yahk)—strong wine
colegio (koh·LAY·jee·oh)—college residence halls
comido (koh·MEED·oh)—dinner, the most important Spanish meal of the day, eaten in mid-afternoon
conquistador (kohn·KEE·stah·dohr)—"conqueror"; term used for the Spanish explorers in the New World
copla (KOH·plah)—short poem set to music
cortado (kohr·TAHD·oh)—"cut"; used to describe expresso with a little milk in it
Covadonga (koh·[b]ah·DOHNG·ah)—cave where Pelayo and his army fought at the beginning of the Reconquest
doctorado (dahk·toh·RAHD·oh)—university degree granted after seven years of study
Don (DOHN)—title of respect for a man
Doña (DOHN·yah)—title of respect for a woman
Euskera (you·SKAY·rah)—ancient Basque language
expresso (ehs·PREHSS·oh)—strong coffee made by quickly forcing boiling water through powderlike dark coffee grounds
Fallas (FEYE·yahss)—festival in Valencia where huge papier-mâché figures are paraded and burned

Feria (fehrr·EE·ah)—festivál of Seville
Finisterre (fihn·iss·TEHR·ray)—Latin for "the end of the earth"
flamenco (flah·MEHN·koh)—Spanish dance featuring quick, clicking steps and handclapping
flan (FLAHN)—custardlike Spanish dessert
Hispania (hiss·PAHN·yah)—Roman name for Spain
Hormiguita (ohr·mee·GWEE·tah)—"Little Ant"; Spanish fairytale character
Inquisition (ihn·kwih·ZIH·shun)—religious court in Spain that tried to purify the Catholic religion
insuficiente (ihn·suh·fiss·see·YEN·tay)—"unsatisfactory"; grade like a *D* in American schools
jai alai (HEYE leye)—fast-paced game played against a wall using a hard rubber ball and catching baskets
jota (HYOH·tah)—folk dance of Aragon
licenciado (lee·sen·see·AH·doh)—university degree given after five years of study
Macarena (mah·kah·RAY·nah), **La**—famous statue in Seville of Our Lady of Hope that is paraded through the city streets
mañana (mahn·YAH·nah)—word meaning "tomorrow"
matador (maht·ah·DOOR)—bullfighter who alone kills the bull at the end of a fight
merienda (mehr·ree·YEHN·dah)—late-afternoon snack
Miguelete (mee·gwehl·LAY·tay), **El**—eight-sided bell tower in Valencia

Moor (MOOR)—Arab people of northwest Africa who ruled Spain for seven hundred years

Moriscos (mohr·ISS·kohs)—descendants of the Moors who changed their religion from Islam to Roman Catholic

muy deficiente (MOOY deh·fiss·ee·YEHN·tay)—"very unsatisfactory"; grade like the American grade *F*

notable (noh·TAH·blay)—"very good"; grade like the American grade *B*

paella (py·AY·yuh)—dish of saffron rice, vegetables, meat, and seafood

paseo (pah·SAY·oh)—traditional Spanish evening walk

patria chica (pah·TREE·uh CHEE·kah)—"little homeland"; phrase referring to the region where a Spaniard was born and raised

pelote (pay·LOH·tay)—another name for jai alai

picador (peek·ah·DOOR)—bullfighters who fight a bull on horseback

porrón (poh·ROHN)—glass wine pitcher with a long spout

Prado (PRAH·doh) **Museum**—large art museum in Madrid

Primera Etapa (pree·MAY·rah eh·TAH·pah)—"first stage"; schools for children ages six through eleven

Puerta del Sol (PWEHR·tah dehl SOHL), **La**—"Gate of the Sun"; plaza in Madrid

rastro (RAHS·troh)—open-air market of Madrid

Ratón Pérez (rah·TOHN PEH·rez)—"Perez the Mouse"; Spanish fairytale character

Romería del Rocío (roh·mehr·REE·ah dehl roh·SEE·oh)—Andalusian festival honoring Our Lady of the Dew

saeta (sy·EH·tah)—"arrow (of prayer)"; short, sad song sung during solemn Holy Week processions

sangría (sahn·GREE·uh)—wine and fruit punch

sardana (sahr·DAH·nah)—folk dance of Catalonia

Segunda Etapa (say·GOON·dah eh·TAH·pah)—"second stage"; schools for children ages twelve to fourteen

sobresaliente(soh·bray·sah·lee·YEN·tay)—"outstanding"; grade like the American grade *A*

sol (SOHL)—sun; sunny

solea (soh·LAY·ah)—type of flamenco

sombra (SOHM·brah)—shade; shady

tapa (TAH·pah)—Spanish appetizer

tertulia (tehr·too·LEE·ah)—talking club that meets in a bar or café

Tortilla Española (tohr·TEE·uh ess·pahn·YOH·lah)—potato and egg omelette

tuna (TOO·nah)—group of young men that serenades young women

turrón (too·RROHN)—hard type of Christmas candy

zarzuela ([th]ar·[TH]WAY·lah)—Spanish opera, often funny, with spoken dialogue

Selected Bibliography

Bristow, Richard. *We Live in Spain.* London: The Bookwright Press, 1984, ©1982.

Cross, Esther and Wilbur. *Spain.* Chicago: Childrens Press, 1985.

Goldston, Robert. *The Siege of the Alcázar.* New York: Franklin Watts, 1972.

______ . *Spain.* New York: Franklin Watts, 1972.

Graham, Robert. *Spain: A Nation Comes of Age.* New York: St. Martin's Press, 1984.

Loder, Dorothy. *The Land and People of Spain* (revised edition). New York: J.B. Lippincott, 1972.

MacKendrick, Paul. *The Iberian Stones Speak: Archaeology in Spain and Portugal.* New York: Funk and Wagnalls, 1969.

Martin, Rupert. *Looking at Spain.* New York: J.B. Lippincott, 1969.

Purcell, Hugh. *The Spanish Civil War.* New York: G.P. Putnam's Sons, 1973.

Spain and Portugal. New York: Silver Burdett, 1986.

Szulc, Tad. *Portrait of Spain.* New York: American Heritage Press, 1972.

Wohl, Gary and Ruibal, Carmen C. *Hispanic Personalities: Celebrities of the Spanish-Speaking World.* New York: Regents Publishing, 1978.

Index

About the Author

Geraldine Woods fell in love with Spain the first time she traveled there, and has since returned several times to visit family friends and to live there for brief periods. Her familiarity with this sunny land inspired her to write *Spain: A Shining New Democracy.*

Ms. Woods has published many books for children on a variety of subjects, sometimes sharing the author billing with her husband, Harold. Among her books are *Bill Cosby: Making America Laugh and Learn, Equal Justice: A Biography of Sandra Day O'Connor*, and *Jim Henson: From Puppets to Muppets.* She is a teacher, and lives with her family in New York City.